3-
7/2021

Rejoicing in Mercy: A Prayer Commentary on the Gospel of Luke

Her neighbors and relatives heard that the Lord had shown his great mercy to Elizabeth, and they rejoiced with her. Luke 1:58

Louis J. Cameli
Archdiocese of Chicago

Rejoicing in Mercy: A Prayer Commentary on the Gospel of Luke
© 2016 Archdiocese of Chicago; 835 N. Rush Street, Chicago, IL 60611. All rights reserved.

To order additional copies please contact the Office for the New Evangelization at 312-534-5299.

Printed in the United States.

ISBN 978-0-9970158-0-5

CONTENTS

FOREWORD

Dear brothers and sisters in Christ,

The joy of the gospel is the recognition of God's mercy at work in our lives and in the world. Luke's account of the gospel of Jesus Christ highlights both the mercy of God and the joy that this mercy ignites in the hearts of believers.

The Gospel according to Luke offers us God's life-giving word, so that we can take it to heart and allow it to enlighten and enliven us. When we hear, read, and pray this Gospel, we can keep in mind the mercy and the joy that it proclaims and let them take root within us.

Together, in this Jubilee of Mercy, let us make this gospel journey and meet Jesus, the face of God's mercy and the source of our joy.

Archbishop Blase J. Cupich
Archbishop of Chicago

INTRODUCTION

When Pope Francis issued *Misericordiae Vultus: Bull of Indiction of the Extraordinary Jubilee of Mercy*, he clearly stated his reason for summoning the Church to observe this jubilee (December 8, 2015—November 20, 2016).

> We need constantly to contemplate the mystery of mercy. It is a wellspring of joy, serenity and peace. Our salvation depends on it. **Mercy:** the word reveals the very mystery of the Most Holy Trinity. **Mercy:** the ultimate and supreme act by which God comes to meet us. **Mercy:** the fundamental law that dwells in the heart of every person who looks sincerely into the eyes of his brothers and sisters on the path of life. **Mercy:** the bridge that connects God and man, opening our hearts to the hope of being loved forever despite our sinfulness.
>
> At times we are called to gaze even more attentively on mercy so that we may become a more effective sign of the Father's action in our lives. For this reason I have proclaimed an Extraordinary Jubilee of Mercy as a special time for the church, a time when the witness of believers might grow stronger and more effective. (nn. 2-3)

A fundamental way "to contemplate the mystery of mercy" is, of course, to turn to the Word of God contained in Sacred Scripture. For the *Jubilee of Mercy,* we are blessed to have the Gospel according to Saint Luke as the gospel for the Sundays of Cycle C which begins with the first Sunday of Advent in November 2015 and concludes on the feast of Christ the King in November 2016. Luke's gospel emphasizes the great theme of God's mercy. This gospel will play an important role in this year of prayer, study, and reflection on God's mercy and our participation in it.

What you have before you is a prayer commentary on Luke's gospel from the perspective of mercy. It is meant to guide prayer and personal reflection with a focus on mercy.

The format follows a set pattern:

- the whole Gospel of Saint Luke is reproduced
- passages that express something about mercy are identified
- an introduction to the passage follows
- a verse or two of the passage is offered for reflection
- a meditation on the passage explains the "mercy meaning"
- a question for reflection follows
- a prayer directs our minds and hearts to the merciful Lord.

This prayer commentary on Luke lends itself to many different uses. Of course, it can be a companion for personal prayer and reflection. It can also be used in small groups and even in classroom settings. The prayer commentary is meant to lead readers, whether individually or in groups, to a personal encounter with God's word and a deeper appreciation of God's mercy fulfilling Pope Francis' hope that we be drawn constantly to contemplate God's mercy.

Fr. Louis J. Cameli

Luke 1

Dedication to Theophilus: 1:1-4

[1]Since many have undertaken to set down an orderly account of the events that have been fulfilled among us, [2]just as they were handed on to us by those who from the beginning were eyewitnesses and servants of the word, [3]I too decided, after investigating everything carefully from the very first,[a] to write an orderly account for you, most excellent Theophilus, [4]so that you may know the truth concerning the things about which you have been instructed.

The Announcement of the Birth of John the Baptist to His Father Zechariah: 1:5-25

[5]In the days of King Herod of Judea, there was a priest named Zechariah, who belonged to the priestly order of Abijah. His wife was a descendant of Aaron, and her name was Elizabeth. [6]Both of them were righteous before God, living blamelessly according to all the commandments and regulations of the Lord. [7]But they had no children, because Elizabeth was barren, and both were getting on in years.

[8]Once when he was serving as priest before God and his section was on duty, [9]he was chosen by lot, according to the custom of the priesthood, to enter the sanctuary of the Lord and offer incense. [10]Now at the time of the incense offering, the whole assembly of the people was praying outside. [11]Then there appeared to him an angel of the Lord, standing at the right side of the altar of incense. [12]When Zechariah saw him, he was terrified; and fear overwhelmed him. [13]But the angel said to him, "Do not be afraid, Zechariah, for your prayer has been heard. Your wife Elizabeth will bear you a son, and you will name him John. [14]You will have joy and gladness, and many will rejoice at his birth, [15]for he will be great in the sight of the Lord. He must never drink wine or strong drink; even before his birth he will be filled with the Holy Spirit. [16]He will turn many of the people of Israel to the Lord their God. [17]With the spirit and power of Elijah he will go before

a   Or *for a long time*

him, to turn the hearts of parents to their children, and the disobedient to the wisdom of the righteous, to make ready a people prepared for the Lord." [18]Zechariah said to the angel, "How will I know that this is so? For I am an old man, and my wife is getting on in years." [19]The angel replied, "I am Gabriel. I stand in the presence of God, and I have been sent to speak to you and to bring you this good news. [20]But now, because you did not believe my words, which will be fulfilled in their time, you will become mute, unable to speak, until the day these things occur."

[21]Meanwhile the people were waiting for Zechariah, and wondered at his delay in the sanctuary. [22]When he did come out, he could not speak to them, and they realized that he had seen a vision in the sanctuary. He kept motioning to them and remained unable to speak. [23]When his time of service was ended, he went to his home.

[24]After those days his wife Elizabeth conceived, and for five months she remained in seclusion. She said, [25]"This is what the Lord has done for me when he looked favorably on me and took away the disgrace I have endured among my people."

The Announcement of the Birth of Jesus to Mary: 1:26-38

[26]In the sixth month the angel Gabriel was sent by God to a town in Galilee called Nazareth, [27]to a virgin engaged to a man whose name was Joseph, of the house of David. The virgin's name was Mary. [28]And he came to her and said, "Greetings, favored one! The Lord is with you."[b] [29]But she was much perplexed by his words and pondered what sort of greeting this might be. [30]The angel said to her, "Do not be afraid, Mary, for you have found favor with God. [31]And now, you will conceive in your womb and bear a son, and you will name him Jesus. [32]He will be great, and will be called the Son of the Most High, and the Lord God will give to him the throne of his ancestor David. [33]He will reign over the house of Jacob forever, and of his kingdom there will be no end." [34]Mary said to the angel, "How can this be, since I am a virgin?"[c] [35]The angel said to her, "The Holy Spirit will come upon you, and

b   Other ancient authorities add *Blessed are you among women*
c   Gk *I do not know a man*

the power of the Most High will overshadow you; therefore
the child to be born[d] will be holy; he will be called Son of
God. [36]And now, your relative Elizabeth in her old age has
also conceived a son; and this is the sixth month for her who
was said to be barren. [37]For nothing will be impossible with
God." [38]Then Mary said, "Here am I, the servant of the Lord;
let it be with me according to your word." Then the angel
departed from her.

The dawn of God's great word of mercy begins in the wombs of
Elizabeth and Mary. Elizabeth conceives her son John who will
announce the coming of the Messiah and prepare a way of repentance
for his coming. Mary conceives Jesus. His very name, which means
"God saves," points to the mercy of God among us. And she can rightly
be called Mother of Mercy.

Mary Visits Elizabeth and Sings God's Praise: 1:39-56

[39]In those days Mary set out and went with haste to a Judean
town in the hill country, [40]where she entered the house of
Zechariah and greeted Elizabeth. [41]When Elizabeth heard
Mary's greeting, the child leaped in her womb. And Elizabeth
was filled with the Holy Spirit [42]and exclaimed with a loud
cry, "Blessed are you among women, and blessed is the fruit
of your womb. [43]And why has this happened to me, that the
mother of my Lord comes to me? [44]For as soon as I heard
the sound of your greeting, the child in my womb leaped for
joy. [45]And blessed is she who believed that there would be[e] a
fulfillment of what was spoken to her by the Lord."

[46]And Mary[f] said, "My soul magnifies the Lord, [47]and my
spirit rejoices in God my Savior, [48]for he has looked with
favor on the lowliness of his servant. Surely, from now on all
generations will call me blessed; [49]for the Mighty One has
done great things for me, and holy is his name. [50]His mercy is
for those who fear him from generation to generation. [51]He
has shown strength with his arm; he has scattered the proud
in the thoughts of their hearts. [52]He has brought down the
powerful from their thrones, and lifted up the lowly; [53]he has

d   Other ancient authorities add *of you*
e   Or *believed, for there will be*
f   Other ancient authorities read *Elizabeth*

filled the hungry with good things, and sent the rich away empty. [54]He has helped his servant Israel, in remembrance of his mercy, [55]according to the promise he made to our ancestors, to Abraham and to his descendants forever." [56]And Mary remained with her about three months and then returned to her home.

Mary and Elizabeth meet each other but, in the Holy Spirit, they encounter the Lord who is deep at work within them through the children they carry. From the fullness of the Spirit within her, Elizabeth cries out a word of blessing directed to her cousin Mary. In turn, Mary filled with the Holy Spirit proclaims: *My soul magnifies the Lord, and my spirit rejoices in God my Savior* (1:46-47). Her song of praise continues to acknowledge the greatness of God and what God has done. Twice she declares the great reach of God's mercy across history and into this very moment of encounter with Elizabeth:

His mercy is for those who fear him from generation to generation. 1:50

He has helped his servant Israel, in remembrance of his mercy, according to the promise he made to our ancestors, to Abraham and to his descendants forever. 1:54-55

Meditation: If we wish to know the breadth and depth of God's mercy in our lives and in the world, we must allow the Holy Spirit to enlighten us. Yes, we allow the Holy Spirit to enter our minds and hearts. The Spirit never imposes on us. We welcome the Holy Spirit by praying earnestly for the gift of the Spirit and removing, as best we can, those obstacles that hinder the Spirit's work within us.

Question: In my life, what are the particular obstacles that I need to remove, so that God's Holy Spirit can work freely within me?

Let us pray: Come, Holy Spirit, fill our minds and hearts as you filled Mary and Elizabeth. Move us to know and to proclaim the great mercy of God, which has touched and changed our lives.

We may forget to be merciful, but God does not forget. His mercy is constant and faithful. *His mercy is for those who fear him from generation to generation.* God remembers his promise of mercy and remains faithful to that promise forever. *He has helped his servant Israel, in remembrance of his mercy, according to the promise he made to our ancestors, to Abraham, and to his descendants forever.* If God remains faithful and remembers across the years his promise of mercy, should we not also always remember his mercy and never let it slip from our awareness?

> **Question:** How can I be mindful and never forgetful of the mercies that God has given me?

> **Let us pray:** God ever-faithful and true, help our forgetful hearts to remember the constancy of your mercy. When we feel lost and alone, stir within us a sense of your unfailing merciful presence.

Zechariah's Prophecy: 1:57-80

[57]Now the time came for Elizabeth to give birth, and she bore a son. [58]Her neighbors and relatives heard that the Lord had shown his great mercy to her, and they rejoiced with her.

[59]On the eighth day they came to circumcise the child, and they were going to name him Zechariah after his father. [60]But his mother said, "No; he is to be called John." [61]They said to her, "None of your relatives has this name." [62]Then they began motioning to his father to find out what name he wanted to give him. [63]He asked for a writing tablet and wrote, "His name is John." And all of them were amazed. [64]Immediately his mouth was opened and his tongue freed, and he began to speak, praising God. [65]Fear came over all their neighbors, and all these things were talked about throughout the entire hill country of Judea. [66]All who heard them pondered them and said, "What then will this child become?" For, indeed, the hand of the Lord was with him.

⁶⁷Then his father Zechariah was filled with the Holy Spirit and spoke this prophecy: ⁶⁸"Blessed be the Lord God of Israel, for he has looked favorably on his people and redeemed them. ⁶⁹He has raised up a mighty savior[g] for us in the house of his servant David, ⁷⁰as he spoke through the mouth of his holy prophets from of old, ⁷¹that we would be saved from our enemies and from the hand of all who hate us. ⁷²Thus he has shown the mercy promised to our ancestors, and has remembered his holy covenant, ⁷³the oath that he swore to our ancestor Abraham, to grant us ⁷⁴that we, being rescued from the hands of our enemies, might serve him without fear, ⁷⁵in holiness and righteousness before him all our days. ⁷⁶And you, child, will be called the prophet of the Most High; for you will go before the Lord to prepare his ways, ⁷⁷to give knowledge of salvation to his people by the forgiveness of their sins. ⁷⁸By the tender mercy of our God, the dawn from on high will break upon[h] us, ⁷⁹to give light to those who sit in darkness and in the shadow of death, to guide our feet into the way of peace." ⁸⁰The child grew and became strong in spirit, and he was in the wilderness until the day he appeared publicly to Israel.

When Zechariah's son John is born and when Zechariah can speak again, the Holy Spirit impels him to speak a prophecy. In the birth of his son and—even more—in the birth of the one whom his son will announce, Zechariah proclaims the great dawn of the mercy of God who has always been faithful to his promise of mercy.

Blessed be the Lord God of Israel…He has raised up a mighty savior for us…Thus he has shown the mercy promised to our ancestors and has remembered his holy covenant…By the tender mercy of our God, the dawn from on high will break upon us, to give light to those who sit in the darkness and in the shadow of death, to guide our feet into the way of peace. (1:68-69, 72, 78-79)

Meditation: John the Baptist is born in unusual circumstances. His parents are older, seemingly unable to conceive. His people live under the shadow of Roman

g   Gk *a horn of salvation*
h   Other ancient authorities read *has broken upon*

rule, and they sense their deep need for renewal—political, moral, and spiritual. His birth signals light beginning to break through darkness.

Question: What is the darkness that I face, a darkness that needs the dawn and light of God's mercy?

Let us pray: O God, ever-faithful and true to your promise of mercy, when we seem to sit in darkness or in the shadow of death, keep us mindful of the breaking dawn of your light, Jesus. In him, let us see the hand of your tender mercy that leads us forward in hope.

Luke 2

The Birth of Jesus: 2:1-21

[1]In those days a decree went out from Emperor Augustus that all the world should be registered. [2]This was the first registration and was taken while Quirinius was governor of Syria. [3]All went to their own towns to be registered. [4]Joseph also went from the town of Nazareth in Galilee to Judea, to the city of David called Bethlehem, because he was descended from the house and family of David. [5]He went to be registered with Mary, to whom he was engaged and who was expecting a child. [6]While they were there, the time came for her to deliver her child. [7]And she gave birth to her firstborn son and wrapped him in bands of cloth, and laid him in a manger, because there was no place for them in the inn.

[8]In that region there were shepherds living in the fields, keeping watch over their flock by night. [9]Then an angel of the Lord stood before them, and the glory of the Lord shone around them, and they were terrified. [10]But the angel said to them, "Do not be afraid; for see—I am bringing you good news of great joy for all the people: [11]to you is born this day in the city of David a Savior, who is the Messiah,[a] the Lord. [12]This will be a sign for you: you will find a child wrapped in bands of cloth and lying in a manger." [13]And suddenly there was with the angel a multitude of the heavenly host,[b] praising God and saying, [14]"Glory to God in the highest heaven, and on earth peace among those whom he favors!"[c]

[15]When the angels had left them and gone into heaven, the shepherds said to one another, "Let us go now to Bethlehem and see this thing that has taken place, which the Lord has made known to us." [16]So they went with haste and found Mary and Joseph, and the child lying in the manger. [17]When they saw this, they made known what had been told them about this child; [18]and all who heard it were amazed at what the shepherds told them. [19]But Mary treasured all these words and pondered them in her heart. [20]The shepherds

a   Or *the Christ*
b   Gk *army*
c   Other ancient authorities read *peace, goodwill among people*

returned, glorifying and praising God for all they had heard and seen, as it had been told them.

[21] After eight days had passed, it was time to circumcise the child; and he was called Jesus, the name given by the angel before he was conceived in the womb.

Jesus is born in poverty. The first people to know him as savior and messiah are poor shepherds. The power of God's mercy takes hold of this world in the poverty of those who know that they can rely on God alone. To those who feel that they are in control of their world or that they can get along quite well on their own, the coming of the merciful savior is invisible. They cannot see him and, even more, they cannot embrace him.

And she gave birth to her firstborn son and wrapped him in bands of cloth, and laid him in a manger, because there was no place for them in the inn. 2:7

In that region there were shepherds living in the fields, keeping watch over their flock by night. Then an angel of the Lord stood before them…the angel said to them…"to you is born this day in the city of David a Savior, who is the Messiah, the Lord." 2:8, 11

Meditation: Only those who know their insufficiency and their need can truly receive God's mercy. If we are satisfied with our lives and ourselves, there is no room to receive what God offers us. If we are fully satisfied, we will have no need for a merciful savior.

Question: How can I count myself among those who are poor and, therefore, disposed to receive the savior?

Let us pray: Grant us, Lord, the grace never to run away from our need and our sense of personal poverty. Enable us to stand before you with Mary, Joseph, and the shepherds as poor people who, in our poverty, can receive the merciful savior born for us.

Jesus in the Temple—Presented and Found: 2:22-52

[22]When the time came for their purification according to the law of Moses, they brought him up to Jerusalem to present him to the Lord [23](as it is written in the law of the Lord, "Every firstborn male shall be designated as holy to the Lord"), [24]and they offered a sacrifice according to what is stated in the law of the Lord, "a pair of turtledoves or two young pigeons."

[25]Now there was a man in Jerusalem whose name was Simeon;[d] this man was righteous and devout, looking forward to the consolation of Israel, and the Holy Spirit rested on him. [26]It had been revealed to him by the Holy Spirit that he would not see death before he had seen the Lord's Messiah.[e] [27]Guided by the Spirit, Simeon[f] came into the temple; and when the parents brought in the child Jesus, to do for him what was customary under the law, [28]Simeon[g] took him in his arms and praised God, saying,

[29]"Master, now you are dismissing your servant[h] in peace, according to your word; [30]for my eyes have seen your salvation, [31]which you have prepared in the presence of all peoples, [32]a light for revelation to the Gentiles and for glory to your people Israel."

[33]And the child's father and mother were amazed at what was being said about him. [34]Then Simeon[i] blessed them and said to his mother Mary, "This child is destined for the falling and the rising of many in Israel, and to be a sign that will be opposed [35]so that the inner thoughts of many will be revealed— and a sword will pierce your own soul too."

[36]There was also a prophet, Anna[j] the daughter of Phanuel, of the tribe of Asher. She was of a great age, having lived with her husband seven years after her marriage, [37]then as a

---

d   Gk *Symeon*
e   Or *the Lord's Christ*
f   Gk *In the Spirit, he*
g   Gk *he*
h   Gk *slave*
i   Gk *Symeon*
j   Gk *Hanna*

widow to the age of eighty-four. She never left the temple but worshiped there with fasting and prayer night and day. [38]At that moment she came, and began to praise God and to speak about the child[k] to all who were looking for the redemption of Jerusalem.

[39]When they had finished everything required by the law of the Lord, they returned to Galilee, to their own town of Nazareth. [40]The child grew and became strong, filled with wisdom; and the favor of God was upon him.

[41]Now every year his parents went to Jerusalem for the festival of the Passover. [42]And when he was twelve years old, they went up as usual for the festival. [43]When the festival was ended and they started to return, the boy Jesus stayed behind in Jerusalem, but his parents did not know it. [44]Assuming that he was in the group of travelers, they went a day's journey. Then they started to look for him among their relatives and friends. [45]When they did not find him, they returned to Jerusalem to search for him. [46]After three days they found him in the temple, sitting among the teachers, listening to them and asking them questions. [47]And all who heard him were amazed at his understanding and his answers. [48]When his parents[l] saw him they were astonished; and his mother said to him, "Child, why have you treated us like this? Look, your father and I have been searching for you in great anxiety." [49]He said to them, "Why were you searching for me? Did you not know that I must be in my Father's house?"[m] [50]But they did not understand what he said to them. [51]Then he went down with them and came to Nazareth, and was obedient to them. His mother treasured all these things in her heart.

[52]And Jesus increased in wisdom and in years,[n] and in divine and human favor.

The temple in Jerusalem was the holy place where heaven and earth intersected. There, God's people went to meet the Lord, and

k   Gk *him*
l   Gk *they*
m   Or *be about my Father's interests?*
n   Or *in stature*

the Lord himself came close to his people. The birth of Jesus, the coming among us of the Word made flesh, now changes the temple. Emmanuel, or God-with-us, enters his temple and claims it as his own. Jesus himself, we come to understand, is the temple of God's merciful presence.

When the time came for their purification according to the law of Moses, they brought him up to Jerusalem to present him to the Lord. 2:22

After three days they found him in the temple, sitting among the teachers, listening to them and asking them questions. 2:46

Meditation: The sacred spaces of our lives remind us of the presence of God. We gather with others in those spaces and call on the name of the Lord. We are mindful of the need to carry the memory of God's mercy across time. We are also mindful to carry his mercy in whatever place we find ourselves. We become the temple of his presence in this world.

Question: What are some of those sacred spaces or sacred times in my life that evoke for me an experience of the merciful presence of God?

Let us pray: Wherever we stand, sit, or walk, let us be a temple of your merciful presence, O Lord. May no place on earth be without your presence, as we strive to carry your word wherever we journey.

Luke 3

The Proclamation of John the Baptist: 3:1-22

¹In the fifteenth year of the reign of Emperor Tiberius, when Pontius Pilate was governor of Judea, and Herod was ruler[a] of Galilee, and his brother Philip ruler[b] of the region of Ituraea and Trachonitis, and Lysanias ruler[c] of Abilene, ²during the high priesthood of Annas and Caiaphas, the word of God came to John son of Zechariah in the wilderness. ³He went into all the region around the Jordan, proclaiming a baptism of repentance for the forgiveness of sins, ⁴as it is written in the book of the words of the prophet Isaiah, "The voice of one crying out in the wilderness: 'Prepare the way of the Lord, make his paths straight. ⁵Every valley shall be filled, and every mountain and hill shall be made low, and the crooked shall be made straight, and the rough ways made smooth; ⁶and all flesh shall see the salvation of God.'"

⁷John said to the crowds that came out to be baptized by him, "You brood of vipers! Who warned you to flee from the wrath to come? ⁸Bear fruits worthy of repentance. Do not begin to say to yourselves, 'We have Abraham as our ancestor'; for I tell you, God is able from these stones to raise up children to Abraham. ⁹Even now the ax is lying at the root of the trees; every tree therefore that does not bear good fruit is cut down and thrown into the fire."

¹⁰And the crowds asked him, "What then should we do?" ¹¹In reply he said to them, "Whoever has two coats must share with anyone who has none; and whoever has food must do likewise." ¹²Even tax collectors came to be baptized, and they asked him, "Teacher, what should we do?" ¹³He said to them, "Collect no more than the amount prescribed for you." ¹⁴Soldiers also asked him, "And we, what should we do?" He said to them, "Do not extort money from anyone by threats or false accusation, and be satisfied with your wages."

a   Gk *tetrarch*
b   Gk *tetrarch*
c   Gk *tetrarch*

¹⁵As the people were filled with expectation, and all were questioning in their hearts concerning John, whether he might be the Messiah,ᵈ ¹⁶John answered all of them by saying, "I baptize you with water; but one who is more powerful than I is coming; I am not worthy to untie the thong of his sandals. He will baptize you withᵉ the Holy Spirit and fire. ¹⁷His winnowing fork is in his hand, to clear his threshing floor and to gather the wheat into his granary; but the chaff he will burn with unquenchable fire."

¹⁸So, with many other exhortations, he proclaimed the good news to the people. ¹⁹But Herod the ruler,ᶠ who had been rebuked by him because of Herodias, his brother's wife, and because of all the evil things that Herod had done, ²⁰added to them all by shutting up John in prison.

²¹Now when all the people were baptized, and when Jesus also had been baptized and was praying, the heaven was opened, ²²and the Holy Spirit descended upon him in bodily form like a dove. And a voice came from heaven, "You are my Son, the Beloved;ᵍ with you I am well pleased."ʰ

The angel of the Lord had announced to Zechariah that his son John would turn many of the people of Israel to the Lord their God and, in the spirit of the prophet Elijah, that he would "make ready a people prepared for the Lord." (1:17) When John begins his ministry in the desert proclaiming a baptism of repentance and preparing a way for the coming of the Lord, people pay attention to him and respond to him. They ask him, "What then should we do?" (3:10) He tells them that the consequence of repentance and the work of preparing for the Lord's coming mean embracing works of mercy and justice in the course of their daily lives.

In reply he said to them, "Whoever has two coats must share with anyone who has none, and whoever has food must do likewise." Even tax collectors came to be baptized, and they asked him, "Teacher, what should we do?"

d   Or *the Christ*
e   Or *in*
f   Gk *tetrarch*
g   Or *my beloved Son*
h   Other ancient authorities read *You are my Son, today I have begotten you*

He said to them, "Collect no more than the amount prescribed for you." Soldiers also asked him, "And we, what should we do?" He said to them, "Do not extort money from anyone by threats or false accusation, and be satisfied with your wages." 3:11-14

Meditation: John the Baptist called his listeners to repentance. Generally, for most of us, repentance means regret for the evil that we have done and a commitment to change our behavior in the future. Certainly, John meant repentance in that sense, but he also meant something more as well. A deep repentance that prepares a way for the Lord and prepares us to receive him—according to John—also includes works of mercy and justice lived out in the course of fulfilling one's daily duties. Repentance, then, means so much more than repenting of past sins. It is a continuing and constructive process framed by mercy and justice.

Question: How do I need to repent and change? How should my repentance be shaped by works of justice and compassion?

Let us pray: Before we call on your mercy, O Lord, help us to embrace mercy in our own lives and in our interactions with others. May our hearts be purified of sin and then made pure by sharing in your compassionate love.

The Ancestors of Jesus: 3:23-38

[23]Jesus was about thirty years old when he began his work. He was the son (as was thought) of Joseph son of Heli, [24]son of Matthat, son of Levi, son of Melchi, son of Jannai, son of Joseph, [25]son of Mattathias, son of Amos, son of Nahum, son of Esli, son of Naggai, [26]son of Maath, son of Mattathias, son of Semein, son of Josech, son of Joda, [27]son of Joanan, son of Rhesa, son of Zerubbabel, son of Shealtiel,[i] son of Neri, [28]son of Melchi, son of Addi, son of Cosam, son of Elmadam,

___
[i]   Gk *Salathiel*

son of Er, [29]son of Joshua, son of Eliezer, son of Jorim, son of Matthat, son of Levi, [30]son of Simeon, son of Judah, son of Joseph, son of Jonam, son of Eliakim, [31]son of Melea, son of Menna, son of Mattatha, son of Nathan, son of David, [32]son of Jesse, son of Obed, son of Boaz, son of Sala,[j] son of Nahshon, [33]son of Amminadab, son of Admin, son of Arni,[k] son of Hezron, son of Perez, son of Judah, [34]son of Jacob, son of Isaac, son of Abraham, son of Terah, son of Nahor, [35]son of Serug, son of Reu, son of Peleg, son of Eber, son of Shelah, [36]son of Cainan, son of Arphaxad, son of Shem, son of Noah, son of Lamech, [37]son of Methuselah, son of Enoch, son of Jared, son of Mahalaleel, son of Cainan, [38]son of Enos, son of Seth, son of Adam, son of God.

j   Other ancient authorities read *Salmon*
k   Other ancient authorities read *Amminadab, son of Aram;* others vary widely

Luke 4

The Temptation of Jesus: 4:1-13

¹Jesus, full of the Holy Spirit, returned from the Jordan and was led by the Spirit in the wilderness, ²where for forty days he was tempted by the devil. He ate nothing at all during those days, and when they were over, he was famished. ³The devil said to him, "If you are the Son of God, command this stone to become a loaf of bread." ⁴Jesus answered him, "It is written, 'One does not live by bread alone.'"

⁵Then the devil[a] led him up and showed him in an instant all the kingdoms of the world. ⁶And the devil[b] said to him, "To you I will give their glory and all this authority; for it has been given over to me, and I give it to anyone I please. ⁷If you, then, will worship me, it will all be yours." ⁸Jesus answered him, "It is written, 'Worship the Lord your God, and serve only him.'"

⁹Then the devil[c] took him to Jerusalem, and placed him on the pinnacle of the temple, saying to him, "If you are the Son of God, throw yourself down from here, ¹⁰for it is written, 'He will command his angels concerning you, to protect you,' ¹¹and 'On their hands they will bear you up, so that you will not dash your foot against a stone.'"

¹²Jesus answered him, "It is said, 'Do not put the Lord your God to the test.'" ¹³When the devil had finished every test, he departed from him until an opportune time.

At his baptism, Jesus was filled with the Holy Spirit. "…the Holy Spirit descended upon him in bodily form like a dove." (3:22) That same Spirit led him "…in the wilderness, where for forty days he was tempted by the devil." (4:1-2) The evil one wants to divert Jesus from his mission as a suffering messiah and loyal son of the Father. The evil one wants him to walk a different path.

a   Gk *he*
b   Gk *he*
c   Gk *he*

He ate nothing at all during those days, and when they were over, he was famished. The devil said to him, "If you are the Son of God, command this stone to become a loaf of bread." 4:2-3

Then the devil…showed him in an instant all the kingdoms of the world… "If you, then, will worship me, it will all be yours." 4:5, 7

Then the devil took him to Jerusalem, and placed him on the pinnacle of the temple, saying to him, "If you are the Son of God, throw yourself down from here…" 4:9

Meditation: Just as the temptations we experience in our own lives have many layers of meaning, so do the temptations of Jesus. If we look on his temptations with the eyes of mercy, we come to understand that not only is the devil trying to divert him from his true mission but, in the process, the devil is also offering him false and self-centered mercies. He is saying: "If you are hungry be kind and merciful to yourself and turn this stone into a loaf of bread. If you want to win the kingdoms of the world, be kind and merciful to yourself and do it easily with a simple act of submission to me. If you want the attention and admiration of the crowd, be kind and merciful to yourself and do it easily by throwing yourself off the pinnacle of the temple and letting God catch you." This is the kind of mercy that the devil offers, and it is thoroughly false and self-centered. Instead of being attuned to the will of God, this false mercy goes after the path of least resistance.

Question: When have I experienced a temptation to embrace a false or easy mercy that is really no mercy at all?

Let us pray: Grant us, O Lord, the spirit of discernment to know the genuine path that leads to you. When we face choices, enable us to see the way of true mercy. As you are steadfast in your mercy, make us faithful not to our comfort but to your holy will.

Jesus at the Beginning of His Ministry in Nazareth 4:14-30

[14]Then Jesus, filled with the power of the Spirit, returned to Galilee, and a report about him spread through all the surrounding country. [15]He began to teach in their synagogues and was praised by everyone.

[16]When he came to Nazareth, where he had been brought up, he went to the synagogue on the sabbath day, as was his custom. He stood up to read, [17]and the scroll of the prophet Isaiah was given to him. He unrolled the scroll and found the place where it was written: [18]"The Spirit of the Lord is upon me, because he has anointed me to bring good news to the poor. He has sent me to proclaim release to the captives and recovery of sight to the blind, to let the oppressed go free, [19]to proclaim the year of the Lord's favor."

[20]And he rolled up the scroll, gave it back to the attendant, and sat down. The eyes of all in the synagogue were fixed on him. [21]Then he began to say to them, "Today this scripture has been fulfilled in your hearing." [22]All spoke well of him and were amazed at the gracious words that came from his mouth. They said, "Is not this Joseph's son?" [23]He said to them, "Doubtless you will quote to me this proverb, 'Doctor, cure yourself!' And you will say, 'Do here also in your hometown the things that we have heard you did at Capernaum.'" [24]And he said, "Truly I tell you, no prophet is accepted in the prophet's hometown. [25]But the truth is, there were many widows in Israel in the time of Elijah, when the heaven was shut up three years and six months, and there was a severe famine over all the land; [26]yet Elijah was sent to none of them except to a widow at Zarephath in Sidon. [27]There were also many lepers[d] in Israel in the time of the prophet Elisha, and none of them was cleansed except Naaman the Syrian." [28]When they heard this, all in the synagogue were filled with rage. [29]They got up, drove him out of the town, and led him to the brow of the hill on which their town was built, so that they might hurl him off the cliff. [30]But he passed through the midst of them and went on his way.

d   The terms *leper* and *leprosy* can refer to several diseases

When Jesus leaves the desert, he returns to his hometown of Nazareth. He goes to the synagogue on the Sabbath and reads from the prophet Isaiah. As he cites the prophet, he speaks about himself and identifies the scope of his mission. He quotes the prophet Isaiah, and he himself assumes the place of a prophet sent by God to bring new life to his people who, as Zechariah said, "sit in darkness and in the shadow of death."(1:79) With Isaiah's words, he names his mission.

The Spirit of the Lord is upon me, because he has anointed me to bring good news to the poor. He has sent me to proclaim release to the captives and recovery of sight to the blind, to let the oppressed go free, to proclaim the year of the Lord's favor. 4:18-19

The eyes of all in the synagogue were fixed on him. Then he began to say to them, "Today this scripture has been fulfilled in your hearing." 4:20-21

Meditation: As we hear Jesus citing these words of Isaiah, we note that there is no mention of the word "mercy," but the reality of mercy permeates the passage. Jesus breaks through the bleak and often despairing condition of the poor with good news that brings hope. He mercifully cuts the shackles of those who are held captive by others or even by their own compulsions. He heals and compassionately restores sight to those who are blind. He graciously lifts up to freedom those who had been pushed down and oppressed. Finally he proclaims the Lord's favor, his grace, his loving mercy freely given. The inspired vision of Isaiah becomes Jesus' mission of mercy. Jesus defines and claims his direction.

Question: Have I really understood Jesus' mission to the world and to me personally as a mission of mercy? Or have I perceived his mission in another way?

Let us pray: Jesus, in the many complications of life, let us keep one thing simple and uncomplicated. Let us daily remember your purpose in coming among us. Let us know your intent to

> share the mercy of God among us. Let us know that your teaching and actions are all directed to bringing that transforming mercy into our shattered and wounded world. Let us simply cling to you and your merciful presence.

Jesus Begins His Ministry of Mercy: 4:31-44

[31]He went down to Capernaum, a city in Galilee, and was teaching them on the sabbath. [32]They were astounded at his teaching, because he spoke with authority. [33]In the synagogue there was a man who had the spirit of an unclean demon, and he cried out with a loud voice, [34]"Let us alone! What have you to do with us, Jesus of Nazareth? Have you come to destroy us? I know who you are, the Holy One of God." [35]But Jesus rebuked him, saying, "Be silent, and come out of him!" When the demon had thrown him down before them, he came out of him without having done him any harm. [36]They were all amazed and kept saying to one another, "What kind of utterance is this? For with authority and power he commands the unclean spirits, and out they come!" [37]And a report about him began to reach every place in the region.

[38]After leaving the synagogue he entered Simon's house. Now Simon's mother-in-law was suffering from a high fever, and they asked him about her. [39]Then he stood over her and rebuked the fever, and it left her. Immediately she got up and began to serve them.

[40]As the sun was setting, all those who had any who were sick with various kinds of diseases brought them to him; and he laid his hands on each of them and cured them. [41]Demons also came out of many, shouting, "You are the Son of God!" But he rebuked them and would not allow them to speak, because they knew that he was the Messiah.[e]

[42]At daybreak he departed and went into a deserted place. And the crowds were looking for him; and when they reached him, they wanted to prevent him from leaving them. [43]But he said to them, "I must proclaim the good news of the

e   Or *the Christ*

kingdom of God to the other cities also; for I was sent for this purpose." [44]So he continued proclaiming the message in the synagogues of Judea.[f]

After Jesus declares his purpose and his mission in Nazareth, he begins to implement it. He casts out an unclean spirit from a man who has been sorely afflicted. He heals Simon's mother-in-law. He lays hands on the many sick people who are brought to him. He presses forward and goes from city to city proclaiming his message of good news.

Jesus rebuked him [the demon], saying, "Be silent, and come out of him!" When the demon had thrown him down before them, he came out of him without having done him any harm. 4:35

Then he stood over her [Simon's mother-in-law] and rebuked the fever, and it left her. 4:39

…all those who had any who were sick with various kinds of diseases brought them to him; and he laid his hands on each of them and cured them. 4:40

"…I must proclaim the good news of the kingdom of God to the other cities…" 4:43

Meditation: When Jesus encounters the people who are brought to him in need of healing—a possessed man, Simon's mother-in-law, the many sick—he sees people whose lives have been taken from them. They are held bound and perhaps even defined by the struggle and the suffering they endure. The maladies have different origins, whether physical or psychological or spiritual, but in a common way they hold people captive. The merciful healing of Jesus frees them to be themselves, as God intended them to be.

Question: What are some of the ways that I have felt bound and unfree? How can God's mercy give me true freedom?

f   Other ancient authorities read *Galilee*

Let us pray: Jesus, bring the healing mercy of God into our lives, so that we can breathe and live and be the ones God intends us to be. Even if our burdens seem to endure, give us a sense of your presence among us and undying hope in your compassionate love.

Luke 5

Jesus Calls the First Disciples: 5:1-11

[1]Once while Jesus[a] was standing beside the lake of Gennesaret, and the crowd was pressing in on him to hear the word of God, [2]he saw two boats there at the shore of the lake; the fishermen had gone out of them and were washing their nets. [3]He got into one of the boats, the one belonging to Simon, and asked him to put out a little way from the shore. Then he sat down and taught the crowds from the boat. [4]When he had finished speaking, he said to Simon, "Put out into the deep water and let down your nets for a catch." [5]Simon answered, "Master, we have worked all night long but have caught nothing. Yet if you say so, I will let down the nets." [6]When they had done this, they caught so many fish that their nets were beginning to break. [7]So they signaled their partners in the other boat to come and help them. And they came and filled both boats, so that they began to sink. [8]But when Simon Peter saw it, he fell down at Jesus' knees, saying, "Go away from me, Lord, for I am a sinful man!" [9]For he and all who were with him were amazed at the catch of fish that they had taken; [10]and so also were James and John, sons of Zebedee, who were partners with Simon. Then Jesus said to Simon, "Do not be afraid; from now on you will be catching people." [11]When they had brought their boats to shore, they left everything and followed him.

When Jesus calls his disciples, when he calls us, he calls us as we are and where we are. He calls the first disciples while they are working as fishermen, as they happen to be washing their nets. They are ordinary people who experience both success and setbacks in their work. Like Peter, they are also very much aware of their own limitations. In his mercy, Jesus sees both them and us as much more than ordinary, limited, and sinful people. Mercy sees in everyone a promise, a hope, and a future.

But when Simon Peter saw it, he fell down at Jesus' knees, saying, "Go away from me, Lord, for I am a sinful man!" 5:8

a   Gk *he*

Then Jesus said to Simon, "Do not be afraid; from now on you will be catching people." 5:10

Meditation: The mystery of our vocation certainly centers on God's desire that we cooperate and collaborate with him for the salvation of the world. Even more mysteriously, however, the omnipotent and transcendent Lord calls us with all our limitations and even in our sinfulness to fulfill holy responsibilities. Our hesitations—"Go away from me"—melt with the Lord's merciful reassurance—"Do not be afraid; from now on you will be catching peopl*e*."

Question: How and why have I hesitated to answer God's call to share his mercy in the world?

Let us pray: When we do not trust ourselves, let us know, O Lord, that you do trust us. When we feel unworthy to do your work or even heed your call, let us know that your merciful love creates a new spirit and a new heart within us. Draw us more deeply into the mystery of our calling and your transforming love.

Jesus Cleanses a Leper and Heals a Paralytic: 5:12-26

[12]Once, when he was in one of the cities, there was a man covered with leprosy.[b] When he saw Jesus, he bowed with his face to the ground and begged him, "Lord, if you choose, you can make me clean." [13]Then Jesus[c] stretched out his hand, touched him, and said, "I do choose. Be made clean." Immediately the leprosy[d] left him. [14]And he ordered him to tell no one. "Go," he said, "and show yourself to the priest, and, as Moses commanded, make an offering for your cleansing, for a testimony to them." [15]But now more than ever the word about Jesus[e] spread abroad; many crowds would gather to hear him and to be cured of their diseases. [16]But he would withdraw to deserted places and pray.

b   The terms *leper* and *leprosy* can refer to several diseases
c   Gk *he*
d   The terms *leper* and *leprosy* can refer to several diseases
e   Gk *him*

[17]One day, while he was teaching, Pharisees and teachers of the law were sitting near by (they had come from every village of Galilee and Judea and from Jerusalem); and the power of the Lord was with him to heal.[f] [18]Just then some men came, carrying a paralyzed man on a bed. They were trying to bring him in and lay him before Jesus;[g] [19]but finding no way to bring him in because of the crowd, they went up on the roof and let him down with his bed through the tiles into the middle of the crowd[h] in front of Jesus. [20]When he saw their faith, he said, "Friend,[i] your sins are forgiven you." [21]Then the scribes and the Pharisees began to question, "Who is this who is speaking blasphemies? Who can forgive sins but God alone?" [22]When Jesus perceived their questionings, he answered them, "Why do you raise such questions in your hearts? [23]Which is easier, to say, 'Your sins are forgiven you,' or to say, 'Stand up and walk'? [24]But so that you may know that the Son of Man has authority on earth to forgive sins"— he said to the one who was paralyzed—"I say to you, stand up and take your bed and go to your home." [25]Immediately he stood up before them, took what he had been lying on, and went to his home, glorifying God. [26]Amazement seized all of them, and they glorified God and were filled with awe, saying, "We have seen strange things today."

Throughout our lives, we make many requests. We hope for a positive response, but we can never be sure. When we call on the mercy of God in faith and trust, it is different. God never turns us down. Even when God's response does not exactly match our initial expectations, we eventually find ourselves blessed well beyond those expectations.

When he saw Jesus, he bowed with his face to the ground and begged him, "Lord, if you choose, you can make me clean." Then Jesus stretched out his hand, touched him, and said, "I do choose. Be made clean." 5:12-13

When Jesus saw their faith, he said, "Friend, your sins are forgiven you." … he said to the one who was paralyzed—"I say to you, stand up and take your bed and go to your home." 5:20, 24

f   Other ancient authorities read *was present to heal them*
g   Gk *him*
h   Gk *into the midst*
i   Gk *Man*

Meditation: Jesus always hears the pleas of those who come to him with faith and trust in his mercy and compassionate love. We are unaccustomed to this kind of unfailing response. In our experience of human love, it seems more conditional and often uncertain. Consistently, the gospel tells us that Jesus never turns anyone away. When we watch Jesus in the gospel, we find ourselves challenged to move similarly with an unfailingly inclusive mercy.

Question: When and why do I hesitate to accept and respond to the pleas of others for mercy?

Let us pray: Good Lord of constant mercy, enable us to be convinced of your steadfast compassion that always hears our pleas. Let us never hesitate to approach you with whatever requests we carry in our hearts. Enable us, then, to live and share that same constant and unfailing mercy with others.

Jesus Calls Levi: 5:27-32

²⁷After this he went out and saw a tax collector named Levi, sitting at the tax booth; and he said to him, "Follow me." ²⁸And he got up, left everything, and followed him.

²⁹Then Levi gave a great banquet for him in his house; and there was a large crowd of tax collectors and others sitting at the table^j with them. ³⁰The Pharisees and their scribes were complaining to his disciples, saying, "Why do you eat and drink with tax collectors and sinners?" ³¹Jesus answered, "Those who are well have no need of a physician, but those who are sick; ³²I have come to call not the righteous but sinners to repentance."

Jesus calls the tax collector Levi and then socializes with him. He does so not to reward Levi's bad behavior. And tax collectors did, indeed, engage in bad behavior. They collaborated with the occupying Roman army, extorted money in the process of collecting legitimate taxes, and

j   Gk *reclining*

bullied people from their position of authority. Jesus does not reward bad behavior. Instead, he summons Levi and others to repentance. Jesus' awareness of his mission to bring God's mercy to people pushes him to the edges of society, where the need is greatest. He moves to the margins without hesitation and in the face of disapproval: *"Why do you eat and drink with tax collectors and sinners?"* (5:30)

Jesus answered, "Those who are well have no need of a physician, but those who are sick; I have come to call not the righteous but sinners to repentance." 5:31

Meditation: The mercy of Jesus intervenes in the lives of people not on the basis of their merits or what they have earned or what they deserve. The mercy of Jesus intervenes on the basis of need. There is a sense of relief in this. We never have to worry about being screened for our worthiness to receive God's mercy. All we have is our need, and that is enough. Our challenge in being merciful to others is the other side of the coin. To walk in the merciful path of Jesus does not mean that we diligently search for worthy recipients of our mercy. Our mercy, like that of Jesus, ought to be directed by the need of the people we serve.

Question: Do I live and act in a way that reflects God's mercy as a sheer gift, nothing that I have earned, deserved, or merited? Why could it be difficult to accept the gift as a gift?

Let us pray: Lead us, Lord, to understand that your mercy always goes to the least deserving, and our mercy must similarly be directed to those who seem to have the weakest claim on us. Let us be at peace with your standards of mercy given and strive to live by them always.

The Question About Fasting: 5:33-39

³³Then they said to him, "John's disciples, like the disciples of the Pharisees, frequently fast and pray, but your disciples eat and drink." ³⁴Jesus said to them, "You cannot make wedding guests fast while the bridegroom is with them, can you? ³⁵The days will come when the bridegroom will be taken away from them, and then they will fast in those days." ³⁶He also told them a parable: "No one tears a piece from a new garment and sews it on an old garment; otherwise the new will be torn, and the piece from the new will not match the old. ³⁷And no one puts new wine into old wineskins; otherwise the new wine will burst the skins and will be spilled, and the skins will be destroyed. ³⁸But new wine must be put into fresh wineskins. ³⁹And no one after drinking old wine desires new wine, but says, 'The old is good.'"ᵏ

k   Other ancient authorities read *better*; others lack verse 39

Luke 6

Questions About the Sabbath and Healing on the Sabbath: 6:1-11

[1]One sabbath[a] while Jesus[b] was going through the grain-fields, his disciples plucked some heads of grain, rubbed them in their hands, and ate them. [2]But some of the Pharisees said, "Why are you doing what is not lawful[c] on the sabbath?" [3]Jesus answered, "Have you not read what David did when he and his companions were hungry? [4]He entered the house of God and took and ate the bread of the Presence, which it is not lawful for any but the priests to eat, and gave some to his companions?" [5]Then he said to them, "The Son of Man is lord of the sabbath."

[6]On another sabbath he entered the synagogue and taught, and there was a man there whose right hand was withered. [7]The scribes and the Pharisees watched him to see whether he would cure on the sabbath, so that they might find an accusation against him. [8]Even though he knew what they were thinking, he said to the man who had the withered hand, "Come and stand here." He got up and stood there. [9]Then Jesus said to them, "I ask you, is it lawful to do good or to do harm on the sabbath, to save life or to destroy it?" [10]After looking around at all of them, he said to him, "Stretch out your hand." He did so, and his hand was restored. [11]But they were filled with fury and discussed with one another what they might do to Jesus.

The Sabbath day of rest was meant to turn the attention of the people of God to the things of God. The Sabbath day of rest also affirmed their dignity. They were no longer slaves but free sons and daughters—members of the household of God.

"Why are you doing what is not lawful on the sabbath?"…Then he said to them, "The Son of Man is lord of the sabbath." 6:2, 5

a   Other ancient authorities read *On the second first sabbath*
b   Gk *he*
c   Other ancient authorities add *to do*

Then Jesus said to them, "I ask you, is it lawful to do good or to do harm on the sabbath, to save life or to destroy it?" 6:9

Meditation: Mercy is not opposed to doing what is lawful. In fact, mercy guarantees that the law will be rightly understood and applied as intended. As Jesus attends to the needs of his disciples for food and of the man with the withered hand for healing, he understands the meaning of the law as honoring God and upholding the dignity of God's people. Genuine mercy is the key. This is not a mercy that gives excuses, but a mercy that wants the law to serve its true purpose.

Question: When I try to observe laws, rules, and expectations, can I move beyond external observance and mere conformity to reach their real purpose in the larger design of God's mercy?

Let us pray: In you, O God righteous and true, mercy and justice can never contradict each other. May our undying commitment to be loyal to you shape and direct us as loyal, faithful, and merciful followers of your Son, Jesus.

Jesus Chooses the Twelve Apostles: 6:12-16

[12]Now during those days he went out to the mountain to pray; and he spent the night in prayer to God. [13]And when day came, he called his disciples and chose twelve of them, whom he also named apostles: [14]Simon, whom he named Peter, and his brother Andrew, and James, and John, and Philip, and Bartholomew, [15]and Matthew, and Thomas, and James son of Alphaeus, and Simon, who was called the Zealot, [16]and Judas son of James, and Judas Iscariot, who became a traitor.

Jesus Teaches and Heals: 6:17-19

[17]He came down with them and stood on a level place, with a great crowd of his disciples and a great multitude of people

from all Judea, Jerusalem, and the coast of Tyre and Sidon. [18]They had come to hear him and to be healed of their diseases; and those who were troubled with unclean spirits were cured. [19]And all in the crowd were trying to touch him, for power came out from him and healed all of them.

Jesus Speaks of Blessings and Woes: 6:20-26

[20]Then he looked up at his disciples and said: "Blessed are you who are poor, for yours is the kingdom of God. [21]"Blessed are you who are hungry now, for you will be filled. "Blessed are you who weep now, for you will laugh. [22]"Blessed are you when people hate you, and when they exclude you, revile you, and defame you[d] on account of the Son of Man. [23]Rejoice in that day and leap for joy, for surely your reward is great in heaven; for that is what their ancestors did to the prophets. [24]"But woe to you who are rich, for you have received your consolation. [25]"Woe to you who are full now, for you will be hungry. "Woe to you who are laughing now, for you will mourn and weep. [26]"Woe to you when all speak well of you, for that is what their ancestors did to the false prophets.

Love for Enemies and Not Judging Others: 6:27-42

[27]"But I say to you that listen, Love your enemies, do good to those who hate you, [28]bless those who curse you, pray for those who abuse you. [29]If anyone strikes you on the cheek, offer the other also; and from anyone who takes away your coat do not withhold even your shirt. [30]Give to everyone who begs from you; and if anyone takes away your goods, do not ask for them again. [31]Do to others as you would have them do to you.

[32]"If you love those who love you, what credit is that to you? For even sinners love those who love them. [33]If you do good to those who do good to you, what credit is that to you? For even sinners do the same. [34]If you lend to those from whom you hope to receive, what credit is that to you? Even sinners lend to sinners, to receive as much again. [35]But love your enemies, do good, and lend, expecting nothing in return.[e] Your

d   Gk *cast out your name as evil*
e   Other ancient authorities read *despairing of no one*

reward will be great, and you will be children of the Most High; for he is kind to the ungrateful and the wicked. [36]Be merciful, just as your Father is merciful.

[37]"Do not judge, and you will not be judged; do not condemn, and you will not be condemned. Forgive, and you will be forgiven; [38]give, and it will be given to you. A good measure, pressed down, shaken together, running over, will be put into your lap; for the measure you give will be the measure you get back."

[39]He also told them a parable: "Can a blind person guide a blind person? Will not both fall into a pit? [40]A disciple is not above the teacher, but everyone who is fully qualified will be like the teacher. [41]Why do you see the speck in your neighbor's[f] eye, but do not notice the log in your own eye? [42]Or how can you say to your neighbor,[g] 'Friend,[h] let me take out the speck in your eye,' when you yourself do not see the log in your own eye? You hypocrite, first take the log out of your own eye, and then you will see clearly to take the speck out of your neighbor's[i] eye.

When Jesus speaks of our relationships with others, he moves us well beyond our ordinary understanding of the logic of relationships. Most human relationships are built on basic reciprocity, a kind of tit-for-tat. Jesus proposes a very different way of living and relating that is centered on mercy and that moves us beyond our ordinary and predictable patterns of relationships.

"But I say to you that listen, Love your enemies, do good to those who hate you, bless those who curse you, pray for those who abuse you." 6:27-28

"Be merciful, just as your Father is merciful." 6:36

"Do not judge, and you will not be judged; do not condemn, and you will not be condemned. Forgive, and you will be forgiven…" 6:37-38

f   Gk *brother's*
g   Gk *brother*
h   Gk *brother*
i   Gk *brother's*

Meditation: When Jesus says, "Love your enemies, do good to those who curse you," he seems to go against every human instinct that pushes us to retaliate against those who do us harm. Retaliation is a proportionate response to those who hurt us. In its place, Jesus calls us to mercy which is essentially disproportionate and beyond our immediate reaction and larger set of inclinations. This kind of merciful response seems to be beyond us, something that we are incapable of. In fact, that is true. It is humanly impossible. That is why he says, "Become merciful, just as your Father is merciful." (6:36) In God, this is possible. But this is a process. In other words, we are becoming merciful people over time if we deliberately commit ourselves to embrace Jesus' words.

To refrain from judging others means that we pull them more and more tightly into the circle of mercy that we have come to embrace. Again, this happens as a process of learning and doing over time.

Question: What might be a particular challenge that I face as I try to become merciful as God is merciful?

> **Let us pray:** Father of mercies, may we never be satisfied with our responses to others, especially to those who harm us. Give us the grace each day to become more like you. Then we will begin to love others as you do and, with that merciful love, bring them to new life.

Actions, Fruits and Proof of a Good, Believing Heart: 6:43-49

[43]"No good tree bears bad fruit, nor again does a bad tree bear good fruit; [44]for each tree is known by its own fruit. Figs are not gathered from thorns, nor are grapes picked from a bramble bush. [45]The good person out of the good treasure of the heart produces good, and the evil person out of evil treasure produces evil; for it is out of the abundance of the heart that the mouth speaks.

⁴⁶"Why do you call me 'Lord, Lord,' and do not do what I tell you? ⁴⁷I will show you what someone is like who comes to me, hears my words, and acts on them. ⁴⁸That one is like a man building a house, who dug deeply and laid the foundation on rock; when a flood arose, the river burst against that house but could not shake it, because it had been well built.ʲ ⁴⁹But the one who hears and does not act is like a man who built a house on the ground without a foundation. When the river burst against it, immediately it fell, and great was the ruin of that house."

Jesus wisely said that good fruit comes from a good tree. A good, believing heart will produce good things, including acts of mercy. Jesus also says that words are insufficient. We can use religious language and call on Jesus by saying "Lord, Lord," but do we really act on his word? Jesus says that hearing and acting on his word is the only solid foundation for our lives. When it is a matter of compassion and mercy, Jesus' words find an echo in the First Letter of John: *Little children, let us love, not in word or speech, but in truth and action. And by this we will know that we are from the truth and will reassure our hearts before him…* (3:18-19)

"No good tree bears bad fruit, nor again does a bad tree bear good fruit; for each tree is known by its own fruit…" 6:43-44

"Why do you call me 'Lord, Lord,' and do not do what I tell you?" 6:46

Meditation: The test of faith's genuineness is not theoretical or how much we know. It is not emotional or how much we feel. It is not verbal or how glib we are in talking about faith. In the end, genuine faith is manifested in listening to the Lord and acting on his word. That fruit comes from the good tree or the good heart. The word he speaks and the action to which he summons us is often about mercy.

ʲ   Other ancient authorities read *founded upon the rock*

Question: Do I regularly measure the truth and authenticity of my faith and my mercy by looking at the fruits of my life and the deeds I have accomplished?

Let us pray: May we always stand ready and attentive, O Lord, to what you say and take it to heart. Then may we bring from our hearts works of mercy and compassion that will honor you and bless our brothers and sisters.

Luke 7

Jesus Heals a Centurion's Servant: 7:1-10

[1]After Jesus[a] had finished all his sayings in the hearing of the people, he entered Capernaum. [2]A centurion there had a slave whom he valued highly, and who was ill and close to death. [3]When he heard about Jesus, he sent some Jewish elders to him, asking him to come and heal his slave. [4]When they came to Jesus, they appealed to him earnestly, saying, "He is worthy of having you do this for him, [5]for he loves our people, and it is he who built our synagogue for us." [6]And Jesus went with them, but when he was not far from the house, the centurion sent friends to say to him, "Lord, do not trouble yourself, for I am not worthy to have you come under my roof; [7]therefore I did not presume to come to you. But only speak the word, and let my servant be healed. [8]For I also am a man set under authority, with soldiers under me; and I say to one, 'Go,' and he goes, and to another, 'Come,' and he comes, and to my slave, 'Do this,' and the slave does it." [9]When Jesus heard this he was amazed at him, and turning to the crowd that followed him, he said, "I tell you, not even in Israel have I found such faith." [10]When those who had been sent returned to the house, they found the slave in good health.

A centurion, a compassionate pagan, is moved by the illness of his servant and seeks out Jesus. He has complete faith and confidence is Jesus. He believes that it is enough for him to make the request of Jesus who can by a word heal his servant. Jesus is amazed at his faith and cures the servant as requested.

The centurion sent his friends to say to him, "Lord, do not trouble yourself, for I am not worthy to have you come under my roof…But only speak the word, and let my servant be healed." 7:6-7

When Jesus heard this he was amazed at him…[and]said ,"I tell you, not even in Israel have I found such faith." 7:9

a   Gk *he*

Meditation: As we listen to this narrative of a merciful centurion who seeks help for his ailing servant, something astonishing happens. The faith of the centurion draws out Jesus' merciful and healing action. Mercy and faith combine to move Jesus to heal the servant. This becomes a powerful model for us. When there are times in which we can do nothing for the people we care about, we place them in God's hands. If we do so from a sense of genuine, compassionate mercy and trusting faith, we can be assured that our prayer will be heard.

Question: When have I had an especially powerful experience of trusting God who is all merciful?

> **Let us pray:** When compassion leads us to see our brothers and sisters in deep need and when we humbly recognize our own inability to help them, enable us to turn to you, O Lord, in sincere faith. Let us be confident that you never turn away those who carry others to you in merciful love.

Jesus Raises the Widow's Son at Nain: 7:11-17

[11]Soon afterwards[b] he went to a town called Nain, and his disciples and a large crowd went with him. [12]As he approached the gate of the town, a man who had died was being carried out. He was his mother's only son, and she was a widow; and with her was a large crowd from the town. [13]When the Lord saw her, he had compassion for her and said to her, "Do not weep." [14]Then he came forward and touched the bier, and the bearers stood still. And he said, "Young man, I say to you, rise!" [15]The dead man sat up and began to speak, and Jesus[c] gave him to his mother. [16]Fear seized all of them; and they glorified God, saying, "A great prophet has risen among us!" and "God has looked favorably on his people!" [17]This word about him spread throughout Judea and all the surrounding country.

b   Other ancient authorities read *Next day*
c   Gk *he*

A widow, probably poor, is on her way to bury her only son, who was a young man. When Jesus sees her accompanied by a large crowd of mourners, Luke says "he had compassion for her." (7:13) In the original Greek, the language that expresses Jesus' reaction is very strong. It might read "he shuddered deep inside of himself" or "he felt in his viscera for her." The point is that the merciful compassion of Jesus in the face of deep human need takes a dramatic and intense form. God's merciful compassion for us is never a detached sense of sympathy or pity. It is always an intense and deeply felt compassion for us in our damaged human condition.

When the Lord saw her, he had compassion for her and said to her, "Do not weep."…And he said, "Young man, I say to you, rise!" …and Jesus gave him to his mother. 7:13-15

Fear seized all of them; and they glorified God, saying, "A great prophet has risen among us!" and "God has looked favorably on his people." 7:16

Meditation: In and through the human heart of Jesus, we know that God is touched by the pain and suffering of our lives. When we experience loss, God knows our loss with a tender and sensitive heart. Once we become aware that we are not alone in our struggle, fear or a reverential awe takes hold of us and we must confess the favor and mercy of God in praise and thanksgiving.

Question: How does it console and encourage me to know that in the human heart of Jesus God knows exactly how I feel, especially in my deepest struggles and most intense pain?

Let us pray: The wonder of your merciful love leads us, O Lord, to confess your greatness. You look on us in our lowliness and stretch out your hand to receive us and hold us. Let us never forget your great mercy. Let our lips never fail to praise you for your goodness to us.

Messengers of John the Baptist Bring Jesus his Question: 7:18-35

[18]The disciples of John reported all these things to him. So John summoned two of his disciples [19]and sent them to the Lord to ask, "Are you the one who is to come, or are we to wait for another?" [20]When the men had come to him, they said, "John the Baptist has sent us to you to ask, 'Are you the one who is to come, or are we to wait for another?'" [21]Jesus[d] had just then cured many people of diseases, plagues, and evil spirits, and had given sight to many who were blind. [22]And he answered them, "Go and tell John what you have seen and heard: the blind receive their sight, the lame walk, the lepers[e] are cleansed, the deaf hear, the dead are raised, the poor have good news brought to them. [23]And blessed is anyone who takes no offense at me."

[24]When John's messengers had gone, Jesus[f] began to speak to the crowds about John:[g] "What did you go out into the wilderness to look at? A reed shaken by the wind? [25]What then did you go out to see? Someone[h] dressed in soft robes? Look, those who put on fine clothing and live in luxury are in royal palaces. [26]What then did you go out to see? A prophet? Yes, I tell you, and more than a prophet. [27]This is the one about whom it is written, 'See, I am sending my messenger ahead of you, who will prepare your way before you.'

[28]I tell you, among those born of women no one is greater than John; yet the least in the kingdom of God is greater than he." [29](And all the people who heard this, including the tax collectors, acknowledged the justice of God,[i] because they had been baptized with John's baptism. [30]But by refusing to be baptized by him, the Pharisees and the lawyers rejected God's purpose for themselves.)

[31]"To what then will I compare the people of this generation, and what are they like? [32]They are like children sitting in the

d   Gk *He*
e   The terms *leper* and *leprosy* can refer to several diseases
f   Gk *he*
g   Gk *him*
h   Or *Why then did you go out? To see someone*
i   Or *praised God*

marketplace and calling to one another, 'We played the flute for you, and you did not dance; we wailed, and you did not weep.'

[33]For John the Baptist has come eating no bread and drinking no wine, and you say, 'He has a demon'; [34]the Son of Man has come eating and drinking, and you say, 'Look, a glutton and a drunkard, a friend of tax collectors and sinners!' [35]Nevertheless, wisdom is vindicated by all her children."

Luke simply says that John the Baptist sent messengers to Jesus to ask him if was the one to come. Matthew's gospel says that John was in prison (Mt 11:2) when he sent his messengers. In either case, John is seeking confirmation that he announced correctly that Jesus was the one "greater than he," the fulfillment of the expectations of the people. Some suggest that John sent his disciples as messengers but for their sake, so that they would be finally convinced that Jesus was indeed the messiah. Others speculate that John was truly and deeply discouraged by his imprisonment and, consequently, had genuine questions about his own mission to prepare a way for the messiah. Whatever the case, John's question becomes an opportunity for Jesus to affirm his mission anew.

So John summoned two of his disciples and sent them to the Lord to ask, "Are you the one who is to come, or are we to wait for another?" 7:18-19

And he [Jesus] answered them, "Go and tell John what you have seen and heard: the blind receive their sight, the lame walk, the lepers are cleansed, the deaf hear, the dead are raised, the poor have good news brought to them. And blessed is anyone who takes no offense at me." 7:22-23

Meditation: Jesus answers John's question by pointing to what he has done. He echoes his words in chapter four of Luke's gospel when he proclaimed his mission in the Nazareth synagogue. In his healing and proclamation of the good news, Jesus brings the compassionate and merciful presence of God to his people. Yes, he is the expected one, the messiah who saves his people by being the merciful face of God.

Question: In my relationship with God, do I allow myself—with John the Baptist—to have questions, hesitations, and struggles?

Let us pray: In the middle of our questions, hesitations, and struggles, help us, O Lord, to remember your compassionate and merciful presence among us. Sustain us in the challenges of our lives with your word of reassurance and your healing work.

A Sinful Woman is Forgiven at the House of Simon the Pharisee: 7:36-50

³⁶One of the Pharisees asked Jesus[j] to eat with him, and he went into the Pharisee's house and took his place at the table. ³⁷And a woman in the city, who was a sinner, having learned that he was eating in the Pharisee's house, brought an alabaster jar of ointment. ³⁸She stood behind him at his feet, weeping, and began to bathe his feet with her tears and to dry them with her hair. Then she continued kissing his feet and anointing them with the ointment. ³⁹Now when the Pharisee who had invited him saw it, he said to himself, "If this man were a prophet, he would have known who and what kind of woman this is who is touching him—that she is a sinner." ⁴⁰Jesus spoke up and said to him, "Simon, I have something to say to you." "Teacher," he replied, "speak." ⁴¹"A certain creditor had two debtors; one owed five hundred denarii,[k] and the other fifty. ⁴²When they could not pay, he canceled the debts for both of them. Now which of them will love him more?" ⁴³Simon answered, "I suppose the one for whom he canceled the greater debt." And Jesus[l] said to him, "You have judged rightly." ⁴⁴Then turning toward the woman, he said to Simon, "Do you see this woman? I entered your house; you gave me no water for my feet, but she has bathed my feet with her tears and dried them with her hair. ⁴⁵You gave me no kiss, but from the time I came in she has not stopped kissing my feet. ⁴⁶You did not anoint my head with oil, but she has

j   Gk *him*
k   The denarius was the usual day's wage for a laborer
l   Gk *he*

anointed my feet with ointment. [47]Therefore, I tell you, her sins, which were many, have been forgiven; hence she has shown great love. But the one to whom little is forgiven, loves little." [48]Then he said to her, "Your sins are forgiven." [49]But those who were at the table with him began to say among themselves, "Who is this who even forgives sins?" [50]And he said to the woman, "Your faith has saved you; go in peace."

In Luke's gospel, Jesus eats with friends, with sinners, and even with his adversaries. The meals become occasions for him to teach and to share the mercy of God. This happens at the house of Simon the Pharisee who invites him in but does not offer him basic hospitality. Instead, a woman known as a sinner stays on the edge of the gathering but washes the feet of Jesus with her tears and anoints them with precious ointment. The contrast is stark between a reluctant and distant host and a woman who draws close to Jesus in intimate gestures of repentance.

"Therefore, I tell you, her sins, which were many, have been forgiven; hence she has shown great love. But the one to whom little is forgiven, loves little." Then he said to her, "Your sins are forgiven…Your faith has saved you, go in peace." 7:47-48, 50

Meditation: The great sign that the mercy of God has touched us is our love. The experience of merciful forgiveness includes a deep sense of being loved by God and that generates our own love in return. That is what happens for the woman in the house of Simon the Pharisee. In the meanwhile, Simon appears to be cold and distant, because he has not let his guest, Jesus, truly enter his home and his heart. Love and mercy are inextricably linked.

Question: Have I fully and completely accepted the fact that by the mercy of God I am really and truly forgiven? Do I embrace this? Do I hesitate?

Let us pray: Break the barriers of our hearts, O Lord, to let your mercy enter. Then, let us find the forgiveness that reshapes our hearts in love. Keep us close to you, and keep us gratefully indebted to your love and mercy.

Luke 8

Some Women Accompany Jesus and Support Him: 8:1-3

[1]Soon afterwards he went on through cities and villages, proclaiming and bringing the good news of the kingdom of God. The twelve were with him, [2]as well as some women who had been cured of evil spirits and infirmities: Mary, called Magdalene, from whom seven demons had gone out, [3]and Joanna, the wife of Herod's steward Chuza, and Susanna, and many others, who provided for them[a] out of their resources.

The Parable of the Sower Presented and Explained: 8:4-15

[4]When a great crowd gathered and people from town after town came to him, he said in a parable: [5]"A sower went out to sow his seed; and as he sowed, some fell on the path and was trampled on, and the birds of the air ate it up. [6]Some fell on the rock; and as it grew up, it withered for lack of moisture. [7]Some fell among thorns, and the thorns grew with it and choked it. [8]Some fell into good soil, and when it grew, it produced a hundredfold." As he said this, he called out, "Let anyone with ears to hear listen!"

[9]Then his disciples asked him what this parable meant. [10]He said, "To you it has been given to know the secrets[b] of the kingdom of God; but to others I speak[c] in parables, so that 'looking they may not perceive, and listening they may not understand.'

[11]"Now the parable is this: The seed is the word of God. [12]The ones on the path are those who have heard; then the devil comes and takes away the word from their hearts, so that they may not believe and be saved. [13]The ones on the rock are those who, when they hear the word, receive it with joy. But these have no root; they believe only for a while and in a time of testing fall away. [14]As for what fell among the thorns, these are the ones who hear; but as they go on their way, they are choked by the cares and riches and pleasures of life, and their

a   Other ancient authorities read *him*
b   Or *mysteries*
c   Gk lacks *I speak*

fruit does not mature. [15]But as for that in the good soil, these are the ones who, when they hear the word, hold it fast in an honest and good heart, and bear fruit with patient endurance.

A Lamp to be Placed on a Lampstand: 8:16-18

[16]"No one after lighting a lamp hides it under a jar, or puts it under a bed, but puts it on a lampstand, so that those who enter may see the light. [17]For nothing is hidden that will not be disclosed, nor is anything secret that will not become known and come to light. [18]Then pay attention to how you listen; for to those who have, more will be given; and from those who do not have, even what they seem to have will be taken away."

The True Kindred of Jesus: 8:19-21

[19]Then his mother and his brothers came to him, but they could not reach him because of the crowd. [20]And he was told, "Your mother and your brothers are standing outside, wanting to see you." [21]But he said to them, "My mother and my brothers are those who hear the word of God and do it."

Jesus Calms a Storm and Calls His Disciples to Faith: 8:22-25

[22]One day he got into a boat with his disciples, and he said to them, "Let us go across to the other side of the lake." So they put out, [23]and while they were sailing he fell asleep. A windstorm swept down on the lake, and the boat was filling with water, and they were in danger. [24]They went to him and woke him up, shouting, "Master, Master, we are perishing!" And he woke up and rebuked the wind and the raging waves; they ceased, and there was a calm. [25]He said to them, "Where is your faith?" They were afraid and amazed, and said to one another, "Who then is this, that he commands even the winds and the water, and they obey him?"

Jesus Heals the Gerasene Demoniac: 8:26-39

[26]Then they arrived at the country of the Gerasenes,[d] which is opposite Galilee. [27]As he stepped out on land, a man of the

---

d   Other ancient authorities read *Gadarenes;* others, *Gergesenes* city who had demons met him. For a long time he had worn[e] no clothes, and he did not live in a house but in the tombs. [28]When he saw Jesus, he fell down before him and shouted at the top of his voice, "What have you to do with me, Jesus, Son of the Most High God? I beg you, do not torment me"— [29]for Jesus[f] had commanded the unclean spirit to come out of the man. (For many times it had seized him; he was kept under guard and bound with chains and shackles, but he would break the bonds and be driven by the demon into the wilds.) [30]Jesus then asked him, "What is your name?" He said, "Legion"; for many demons had entered him. [31]They begged him not to order them to go back into the abyss.

[32]Now there on the hillside a large herd of swine was feeding; and the demons[g] begged Jesus[h] to let them enter these. So he gave them permission. [33]Then the demons came out of the man and entered the swine, and the herd rushed down the steep bank into the lake and was drowned.

[34]When the swineherds saw what had happened, they ran off and told it in the city and in the country. [35]Then people came out to see what had happened, and when they came to Jesus, they found the man from whom the demons had gone sitting at the feet of Jesus, clothed and in his right mind. And they were afraid. [36]Those who had seen it told them how the one who had been possessed by demons had been healed. [37]Then all the people of the surrounding country of the Gerasenes[i] asked Jesus[j] to leave them; for they were seized with great fear. So he got into the boat and returned. [38]The man from whom the demons had gone begged that he might be with him; but Jesus[k] sent him away, saying, [39]"Return to your home, and declare how much God has done for you." So he went away, proclaiming throughout the city how much Jesus had done for him.

---

e   Other ancient authorities read *a man of the city who had had demons for a long time met him.*
f   Gk *he*
g   Gk *they*
h   Gk *him*
i   Other ancient authorities read *Gadarenes*; others, *Gergesenes*
j   Gk *him*
k   Gk *he*

When Jesus meets the Gerasene demoniac, he encounters a tortured person who is held bound by the demons within him. The man is alienated and separated from those in his own town. And, even more, he is unable to ask for help. Jesus, in a great act of mercy, frees the man from what oppresses him.

Then people came out to see what had happened, and when they came to Jesus, they found the man from whom the demons had gone sitting at the feet of Jesus, clothed and in his right mind. And they were afraid. 8:35

The man from whom the demons had gone begged that he might be with him; but Jesus sent him away, saying, "Return to your home, and declare how much God has done for you." So he went away, proclaiming throughout the city how much Jesus had done for him. 8:38-39

Meditation: When the mercy of God touches us, as it did the Gerasene demoniac, we are transformed. We cannot simply rest in that great change. Like the healed man of the gospel, we have a call to proclaim what God has done, to give witness to the merciful action of God in our lives. This echoes Mary's song, the Magnificat, in which she declares what God, in his great mercy, has accomplished.

Question: How readily do I share what God in his great mercy has accomplished in me? Am I hesitant to share that? If so, why?

Let us pray: When your mercy touches and heals our lives, O Lord, keep us grateful. Even more, enable us to praise your name and declare what you have done before all people. Make us faithful witnesses of your love, power, and mercy.

A Little Girl Restored to Life and a Woman Healed of a Long Illness: 8:40-56

[40]Now when Jesus returned, the crowd welcomed him, for they were all waiting for him. [41]Just then there came a man named Jairus, a leader of the synagogue. He fell at Jesus' feet

and begged him to come to his house, [42]for he had an only daughter, about twelve years old, who was dying. As he went, the crowds pressed in on him. [43]Now there was a woman who had been suffering from hemorrhages for twelve years; and though she had spent all she had on physicians,[1] no one could cure her. [44]She came up behind him and touched the fringe of his clothes, and immediately her hemorrhage stopped. [45]Then Jesus asked, "Who touched me?" When all denied it, Peter[m] said, "Master, the crowds surround you and press in on you." [46]But Jesus said, "Someone touched me; for I noticed that power had gone out from me." [47]When the woman saw that she could not remain hidden, she came trembling; and falling down before him, she declared in the presence of all the people why she had touched him, and how she had been immediately healed. [48]He said to her, "Daughter, your faith has made you well; go in peace."

[49]While he was still speaking, someone came from the leader's house to say, "Your daughter is dead; do not trouble the teacher any longer." [50]When Jesus heard this, he replied, "Do not fear. Only believe, and she will be saved." [51]When he came to the house, he did not allow anyone to enter with him, except Peter, John, and James, and the child's father and mother. [52]They were all weeping and wailing for her; but he said, "Do not weep; for she is not dead but sleeping." [53]And they laughed at him, knowing that she was dead. [54]But he took her by the hand and called out, "Child, get up!" [55]Her spirit returned, and she got up at once. Then he directed them to give her something to eat. [56]Her parents were astounded; but he ordered them to tell no one what had happened.

The mercy of God cuts through seemingly impossible situations and then brings new life to people. This happens in the intertwined stories of a little dying girl and a long-suffering woman. Jesus goes to the house of Jairus to save his daughter. He snatches her from death and restores her to her parents. On his way to the house, a desperately and chronically ill woman touches a fringe of Jesus' clothing and finds

---

l   Other ancient authorities lack *and though she had spent all she had on physicians*
m   Other ancient authorities add *and those who were with him*

herself healed. For God's mercy, there is no obstacle strong enough to block its saving and healing power.

…she declared in the presence of all the people why she had touched him, and how she had been immediately healed. He said to her, "Daughter, your faith has made you well; go in peace." 8:47-48

While he was still speaking, someone came from the leader's house to say, "Your daughter is dead; do not trouble the teacher any longer." When Jesus heard this, he replied, "Do not fear. Only believe, and she will be saved." 8:49-50

Meditation: The power of God's mercy is limitless. That is certain and clear. The question is: Will we—through faith and trust—allow that powerful mercy to take hold of our lives? The chronically ill woman did, and so did Jairus. In that act of faith and trust, we surrender ourselves into God's hands, and we allow God to take the lead.

Question: How do I still need to learn the way of surrendering to the mercy of God? Why is surrendering so challenging for me?

Let us pray: Firm up our faith, O Lord, so that we may never doubt the power of your mercy to untie the impossible knots of our lives. Enable us to encourage others with the same confidence in your powerful mercy.

Luke 9

The Mission of the Twelve: 9:1-6

> [1]Then Jesus[a] called the twelve together and gave them power and authority over all demons and to cure diseases, [2]and he sent them out to proclaim the kingdom of God and to heal. [3]He said to them, "Take nothing for your journey, no staff, nor bag, nor bread, nor money—not even an extra tunic. [4]Whatever house you enter, stay there, and leave from there. [5]Wherever they do not welcome you, as you are leaving that town shake the dust off your feet as a testimony against them." [6]They departed and went through the villages, bringing the good news and curing diseases everywhere.

Jesus extends his mission of mercy through the twelve disciples who form the inner core of his followers. He sends them on a trial run of the mission he will entrust to them. He empowers them to do the very same things that he came to do—to proclaim the kingdom, to heal, and to cast out unclean spirits.

Then Jesus called the twelve together and gave them power and authority over all demons and to cure diseases, and he sent them out to proclaim the kingdom of God and to heal. 9:1-2

They departed and went through the villages, bringing the good news and curing diseases everywhere. 9:6

Meditation: God uses limited and often sinful human beings for his divine purposes. The twelve disciples whom Jesus sends in mission are far from perfect. It makes no difference. They share in his mission of mercy not because of their abilities or virtues but because he enables and sends them. A similar thing happens for us.

Question: Am I consciously aware that I have a mission to bring the mercy of God to the world? If not, what blocks that awareness?

a   Gk *he*

Let us pray: In your mysterious designs, O God of mercy, you call us to share in the mission of Jesus. We are to be instruments of your mercy as we proclaim good news, heal those in need, and forgive others. Keep us mindful of the great purpose you have given to us, and make us ready with unstinting generosity to fulfill your will.

Herod is Perplexed: 9:7-9

[7]Now Herod the ruler[b] heard about all that had taken place, and he was perplexed, because it was said by some that John had been raised from the dead, [8]by some that Elijah had appeared, and by others that one of the ancient prophets had arisen. [9]Herod said, "John I beheaded; but who is this about whom I hear such things?" And he tried to see him.

Jesus Feeds the Five Thousand: 9:10-17

[10]On their return the apostles told Jesus[c] all they had done. He took them with him and withdrew privately to a city called Bethsaida. [11]When the crowds found out about it, they followed him; and he welcomed them, and spoke to them about the kingdom of God, and healed those who needed to be cured.

[12]The day was drawing to a close, and the twelve came to him and said, "Send the crowd away, so that they may go into the surrounding villages and countryside, to lodge and get provisions; for we are here in a deserted place." [13]But he said to them, "You give them something to eat." They said, "We have no more than five loaves and two fish—unless we are to go and buy food for all these people." [14]For there were about five thousand men. And he said to his disciples, "Make them sit down in groups of about fifty each." [15]They did so and made them all sit down. [16]And taking the five loaves and the two fish, he looked up to heaven, and blessed and broke them, and gave them to the disciples to set before the crowd. [17]And

b   Gk *tetrarch*
c   Gk *him*

all ate and were filled. What was left over was gathered up, twelve baskets of broken pieces.

Jesus brings mercy to this world. It is powerful and mysterious. It is also very simple and direct in addressing basic human needs. The crowds who accompany him are hungry. He feeds them. Mercy comes to the crowds through a few loaves and fish.

"You give them something to eat." 9:13

And taking the five loaves and the two fish, he looked up to heaven, and blessed and broke them, and gave them to the disciples to set before the crowd. And all ate and were filled. 9:16-17

> **Meditation**: God's mercy meets human needs. When we walk in the footsteps of Jesus and meet human needs, we make God's mercy present in the world. There is nothing elaborate or complicated in feeding those who hunger. That is the path that God's mercy takes in this world and, now, through us.
>
> **Question:** Do I regularly scan this world to see the needs that mercy can meet? Am I more often caught up in my own preoccupations?
>
> **Let us pray:** Bring us to acknowledge the little ways of your mercy, O Lord, so that we may always be alert to the needs of our brothers and sisters and always ready to serve them in their needs, great and small.

Peter's Profession of Jesus Who Foretells His Death and Resurrection: 9:18-27

[18]Once when Jesus[d] was praying alone, with only the disciples near him, he asked them, "Who do the crowds say that I am?" [19]They answered, "John the Baptist; but others, Elijah; and still others, that one of the ancient prophets has arisen."

d   Gk *he*

²⁰He said to them, "But who do you say that I am?" Peter answered, "The Messiah^e of God."

²¹He sternly ordered and commanded them not to tell anyone, ²²saying, "The Son of Man must undergo great suffering, and be rejected by the elders, chief priests, and scribes, and be killed, and on the third day be raised."

²³Then he said to them all, "If any want to become my followers, let them deny themselves and take up their cross daily and follow me. ²⁴For those who want to save their life will lose it, and those who lose their life for my sake will save it. ²⁵What does it profit them if they gain the whole world, but lose or forfeit themselves? ²⁶Those who are ashamed of me and of my words, of them the Son of Man will be ashamed when he comes in his glory and the glory of the Father and of the holy angels. ²⁷But truly I tell you, there are some standing here who will not taste death before they see the kingdom of God."

The Transfiguration of Jesus Before His Disciples: 9:28-36

²⁸Now about eight days after these sayings Jesus^f took with him Peter and John and James, and went up on the mountain to pray. ²⁹And while he was praying, the appearance of his face changed, and his clothes became dazzling white. ³⁰Suddenly they saw two men, Moses and Elijah, talking to him. ³¹They appeared in glory and were speaking of his departure, which he was about to accomplish at Jerusalem. ³²Now Peter and his companions were weighed down with sleep; but since they had stayed awake,^g they saw his glory and the two men who stood with him. ³³Just as they were leaving him, Peter said to Jesus, "Master, it is good for us to be here; let us make three dwellings,^h one for you, one for Moses, and one for Elijah"—not knowing what he said. ³⁴While he was saying this, a cloud came and overshadowed them; and they were terrified as they entered the cloud. ³⁵Then from the cloud came a voice that said, "This is my Son,

---

e   Or *The Christ*
f   Gk *he*
g   Or *but when they were fully awake*
h   Or *tents*

my Chosen;[i] listen to him!" [36]When the voice had spoken, Jesus was found alone. And they kept silent and in those days told no one any of the things they had seen.

Jesus Heals a Boy with a Demon: 9:37-43

[37]On the next day, when they had come down from the mountain, a great crowd met him. [38]Just then a man from the crowd shouted, "Teacher, I beg you to look at my son; he is my only child. [39]Suddenly a spirit seizes him, and all at once he[j] shrieks. It convulses him until he foams at the mouth; it mauls him and will scarcely leave him. [40]I begged your disciples to cast it out, but they could not." [41]Jesus answered, "You faithless and perverse generation, how much longer must I be with you and bear with you? Bring your son here." [42]While he was coming, the demon dashed him to the ground in convulsions. But Jesus rebuked the unclean spirit, healed the boy, and gave him back to his father. [43]And all were astounded at the greatness of God.

One of the frequent refrains in the Psalms is "The Lord hears the cry of the poor." In this passage, a poor man begs Jesus to heal his son. We know that God is close to those who suffer. When we call on his mercy, he answers without fail.

"Teacher, I beg you to look at my son; he is my only child. Suddenly a spirit seizes him…it mauls him and will scarcely leave him." 9:38-39

But Jesus rebuked the unclean spirit, healed the boy, and gave him back to his father. 9:42

Meditation: The prayer of a desperate parent comes straight from the heart. It is focused. It is urgent. This is the kind of prayer that God's mercy finds irresistible. Jesus restores the child whole and healthy to his father.

Question: When has my prayer for God's mercy been urgent? How was I heard?

i   Other ancient authorities read *my Beloved*
j   Or *it*

> **Let us pray:** O God of compassion, teach us to cry out to you with our most urgent needs. Let us know how your unfailing mercy wants to heal us and restore us.

Jesus Again Foretells His Death: 9:44-48

While everyone was amazed at all that he was doing, he said to his disciples, [44]"Let these words sink into your ears: The Son of Man is going to be betrayed into human hands." [45]But they did not understand this saying; its meaning was concealed from them, so that they could not perceive it. And they were afraid to ask him about this saying.

[46]An argument arose among them as to which one of them was the greatest. [47]But Jesus, aware of their inner thoughts, took a little child and put it by his side, [48]and said to them, "Whoever welcomes this child in my name welcomes me, and whoever welcomes me welcomes the one who sent me; for the least among all of you is the greatest."

An Exorcist Not in the Company of Jesus: 9:49-50

[49]John answered, "Master, we saw someone casting out demons in your name, and we tried to stop him, because he does not follow with us." [50]But Jesus said to him, "Do not stop him; for whoever is not against you is for you."

A Samaritan Village Refuses to Receive Jesus: 9:51-56

[51]When the days drew near for him to be taken up, he set his face to go to Jerusalem. [52]And he sent messengers ahead of him. On their way they entered a village of the Samaritans to make ready for him; [53]but they did not receive him, because his face was set toward Jerusalem. [54]When his disciples James and John saw it, they said, "Lord, do you want us to command fire to come down from heaven and consume them?"[k] [55]But he turned and rebuked them. [56]Then[l] they went on to another village.

---

k   Other ancient authorities add *as Elijah did*
l   Other ancient authorities read *rebuked them, and said, "You do not know what spirit you are of, 56for the Son of Man has not come to destroy the lives of human beings but to save them." Then*

Those Who Want to be the Followers of Jesus: 9:57-62

[57]As they were going along the road, someone said to him, "I will follow you wherever you go." [58]And Jesus said to him, "Foxes have holes, and birds of the air have nests; but the Son of Man has nowhere to lay his head." [59]To another he said, "Follow me." But he said, "Lord, first let me go and bury my father." [60]But Jesus[m] said to him, "Let the dead bury their own dead; but as for you, go and proclaim the kingdom of God." [61]Another said, "I will follow you, Lord; but let me first say farewell to those at my home." [62]Jesus said to him, "No one who puts a hand to the plow and looks back is fit for the kingdom of God."

The demands of following Jesus, as he explains them, are very challenging. There seems to be no room for compassion or even for merciful accommodation.

To another he said, "Follow me." But he said, "Lord, first let me go and bury my father." But Jesus said to him, "Let the dead bury their own dead; but as for you, go and proclaim the kingdom of God." 9:59-60

Meditation: Luke's gospel underscores, in an uncompromising way, the demands of following Jesus. These demands do seem to be extreme. Their harshness seems to leave behind any sense of mercy. In fact, that is not true. The call—*Follow me*—puts the focus and the priority on Jesus, the source of mercy. What we must leave behind are our designs for how we think we can fulfill our summons to mercy and compassion. In the end, we find true mercy only in him, not in our own plans.

Question: Am I able to focus my life on the merciful Jesus? If not, what keeps me from that focus?

Let us pray: Grant us, O Lord, detachment from our own plans and designs that obstruct and impede our response to your call. Make us open

m   Gk *he*

to your will and path by setting and keeping our focus on your son Jesus, who is the true source and sure direction for our sharing in your mercy.

Luke 10

The Mission of the Seventy Disciples and Their Return in Joy: 10:1-24

[1]After this the Lord appointed seventy[a] others and sent them on ahead of him in pairs to every town and place where he himself intended to go. [2]He said to them, "The harvest is plentiful, but the laborers are few; therefore ask the Lord of the harvest to send out laborers into his harvest. [3]Go on your way. See, I am sending you out like lambs into the midst of wolves. [4]Carry no purse, no bag, no sandals; and greet no one on the road. [5]Whatever house you enter, first say, 'Peace to this house!' [6]And if anyone is there who shares in peace, your peace will rest on that person; but if not, it will return to you. [7]Remain in the same house, eating and drinking whatever they provide, for the laborer deserves to be paid. Do not move about from house to house. [8]Whenever you enter a town and its people welcome you, eat what is set before you; [9]cure the sick who are there, and say to them, 'The kingdom of God has come near to you.'[b] [10]But whenever you enter a town and they do not welcome you, go out into its streets and say, [11]'Even the dust of your town that clings to our feet, we wipe off in protest against you. Yet know this: the kingdom of God has come near.'[c] [12]I tell you, on that day it will be more tolerable for Sodom than for that town.

[13]"Woe to you, Chorazin! Woe to you, Bethsaida! For if the deeds of power done in you had been done in Tyre and Sidon, they would have repented long ago, sitting in sackcloth and ashes. [14]But at the judgment it will be more tolerable for Tyre and Sidon than for you. [15]And you, Capernaum, will you be exalted to heaven? No, you will be brought down to Hades.

[16]"Whoever listens to you listens to me, and whoever rejects you rejects me, and whoever rejects me rejects the one who sent me."

---

a   Other ancient authorities read *seventy-two*
b   Or *is at hand for you*
c   Or *is at hand*

¹⁷The seventy^d returned with joy, saying, "Lord, in your name even the demons submit to us!" ¹⁸He said to them, "I watched Satan fall from heaven like a flash of lightning. ¹⁹See, I have given you authority to tread on snakes and scorpions, and over all the power of the enemy; and nothing will hurt you. ²⁰Nevertheless, do not rejoice at this, that the spirits submit to you, but rejoice that your names are written in heaven."

²¹At that same hour Jesus^e rejoiced in the Holy Spirit^f and said, "I thank^g you, Father, Lord of heaven and earth, because you have hidden these things from the wise and the intelligent and have revealed them to infants; yes, Father, for such was your gracious will.^h ²²All things have been handed over to me by my Father; and no one knows who the Son is except the Father, or who the Father is except the Son and anyone to whom the Son chooses to reveal him."

²³Then turning to the disciples, Jesusⁱ said to them privately, "Blessed are the eyes that see what you see! ²⁴For I tell you that many prophets and kings desired to see what you see, but did not see it, and to hear what you hear, but did not hear it."

The Parable of the Good Samaritan: 10:25-37

²⁵Just then a lawyer stood up to test Jesus.^j "Teacher," he said, "what must I do to inherit eternal life?" ²⁶He said to him, "What is written in the law? What do you read there?" ²⁷He answered, "You shall love the Lord your God with all your heart, and with all your soul, and with all your strength, and with all your mind; and your neighbor as yourself." ²⁸And he said to him, "You have given the right answer; do this, and you will live."

²⁹But wanting to justify himself, he asked Jesus, "And who is my neighbor?" ³⁰Jesus replied, "A man was going down from Jerusalem to Jericho, and fell into the hands of robbers, who

d   Other ancient authorities read *seventy-two*
e   Gk *he*
f   Other authorities read *in the spirit*
g   Or *praise*
h   Or *for so it was well-pleasing in your sight*
i   Gk *he*
j   Gk *him*

stripped him, beat him, and went away, leaving him half dead. [31]Now by chance a priest was going down that road; and when he saw him, he passed by on the other side. [32]So likewise a Levite, when he came to the place and saw him, passed by on the other side. [33]But a Samaritan while traveling came near him; and when he saw him, he was moved with pity. [34]He went to him and bandaged his wounds, having poured oil and wine on them. Then he put him on his own animal, brought him to an inn, and took care of him. [35]The next day he took out two denarii,[k] gave them to the innkeeper, and said, 'Take care of him; and when I come back, I will repay you whatever more you spend.' [36]Which of these three, do you think, was a neighbor to the man who fell into the hands of the robbers?" [37]He said, "The one who showed him mercy." Jesus said to him, "Go and do likewise."

The parable of the Good Samaritan, a story of mercy and compassion, is unique to Luke's gospel. This beautiful story begins with a lawyer's attempt to test the Lord. Jesus, then, does not so much argue a case as illustrate the mercy and compassion that alone can give life.

"Teacher…what must I do to inherit eternal life?"… He answered, "You shall love the Lord your God with all your heart…and your neighbor as yourself." …he asked Jesus, "And who is my neighbor?" 10:25, 27, 29

"But a Samaritan while travelling came near him; and when he saw him, he was moved with pity. He went to him and bandaged his wounds… Which of these three do you think was a neighbor to the man who fell into the hands of the robbers?...The one who showed him mercy." 10:33-34, 36-37

Meditation: The touching story of the Good Samaritan with its wonderful details can obscure the fact that it is a response to an all-important question: What must I do to inherit eternal life? The path to eternal life is a path that "shows mercy" to others. Much more important than avoiding the violation of rules or fulfilling particular religious precepts—as important as these are— is a life of compassion and mercy directed toward others. That is the

[k]   The denarius was the usual day's wage for a laborer

key to eternal life.

Question: How can I train my eyes to see others in the mercy of God so that I come to know them as my neighbor?

> **Let us pray:** In your kindness, O Lord, help us to see others as you see them—in need of our help and mercy. May our lives be guided and measured by the merciful compassion we have for others.

Jesus Visits Martha and Mary: 10:38-42

[38]Now as they went on their way, he entered a certain village, where a woman named Martha welcomed him into her home. [39]She had a sister named Mary, who sat at the Lord's feet and listened to what he was saying. [40]But Martha was distracted by her many tasks; so she came to him and asked, "Lord, do you not care that my sister has left me to do all the work by myself? Tell her then to help me." [41]But the Lord answered her, "Martha, Martha, you are worried and distracted by many things; [42]there is need of only one thing.[1] Mary has chosen the better part, which will not be taken away from her."

[1]   Other ancient authorities read *few things are necessary, or only one*

Luke 11

Jesus Teaches the Lord's Prayer and Perseverance in Prayer: 11:1-13

¹He was praying in a certain place, and after he had finished, one of his disciples said to him, "Lord, teach us to pray, as John taught his disciples." ²He said to them, "When you pray, say: Father,ᵃ hallowed be your name. Your kingdom come.ᵇ ³Give us each day our daily bread.ᶜ ⁴And forgive us our sins, for we Ourselves forgive everyone indebted to us. And do not bring us to the time of trial."ᵈ

⁵And he said to them, "Suppose one of you has a friend, and you go to him at midnight and say to him, 'Friend, lend me three loaves of bread; ⁶for a friend of mine has arrived, and I have nothing to set before him.' ⁷And he answers from within, 'Do not bother me; the door has already been locked, and my children are with me in bed; I cannot get up and give you anything.' ⁸I tell you, even though he will not get up and give him anything because he is his friend, at least because of his persistence he will get up and give him whatever he needs.

⁹"So I say to you, Ask, and it will be given you; search, and you will find; knock, and the door will be opened for you. ¹⁰For everyone who asks receives, and everyone who searches finds, and for everyone who knocks, the door will be opened. ¹¹Is there anyone among you who, if your child asks forᵉ a fish, will give a snake instead of a fish? ¹²Or if the child asks for an egg, will give a scorpion? ¹³If you then, who are evil, know how to give good gifts to your children, how much more will the heavenly Father give the Holy Spiritᶠ to those who ask him!"

When Jesus' disciples ask him to teach them how to pray, he does more than just offer them a formula. He gives them a way of living their

a   Other ancient authorities read *Our Father in heaven*
b   A few ancient authorities read *Your Holy Spirit come upon us and cleanse us.* Other ancient authorities add *Your will be done, on earth as in heaven*
c   Or *our bread for tomorrow*
d   Or *us into temptation.* Other ancient authorities add *but rescue us from the evil one* (or *from evil*)
e   Other ancient authorities add *bread, will give a stone; or if your child asks for*
f   Other ancient authorities read *the Father gives the Holy Spirit from heaven*

prayer and a way of living with great expectations. Not surprisingly, all this has to do with his constant concern for mercy.

He said to them, "When you pray, say...'And forgive us our sins, for we ourselves forgive everyone indebted to us.'" 11:2, 4

"If you then, who are evil, know how to give good gifts to your children, how much more will the heavenly Father give the Holy Spirit to those who ask him!" 11:13

Meditation: The merciful forgiveness for which we pray must also be the pattern of our lives and interactions with others. A prayer for mercy assumes that we also take responsibility for mercy.

Our own mercy and care for those we love, such as our children, can be real and true. At the same time, it remains a mere shadow and a slight intimation of the boundless mercy that God gives us when we ask. Our prayer for mercy must be built on our great expectations of God, which we rightly have.

Question: If I pray for mercy, what is the best way for me to take responsibility for mercy in my interactions with others? How can I always link my prayer for mercy with my commitment to act mercifully?

Let us pray: Teach our hearts to pray, O Lord, so that what we ask for, we may also share with others. Teach our hearts to pray, O Lord, so that our hope in you may always exceed what we can imagine. Let us ask for mercy and share mercy. Let us wait confidently for your mercy, which is beyond measure.

Jesus and Beelzebul, Confusing Good and Evil: 11:14-23

[14]Now he was casting out a demon that was mute; when the demon had gone out, the one who had been mute spoke, and

the crowds were amazed. [15]But some of them said, "He casts out demons by Beelzebul, the ruler of the demons." [16]Others, to test him, kept demanding from him a sign from heaven. [17]But he knew what they were thinking and said to them, "Every kingdom divided against itself becomes a desert, and house falls on house. [18]If Satan also is divided against himself, how will his kingdom stand? —for you say that I cast out the demons by Beelzebul. [19]Now if I cast out the demons by Beelzebul, by whom do your exorcists[g] cast them out? Therefore they will be your judges. [20]But if it is by the finger of God that I cast out the demons, then the kingdom of God has come to you. [21]When a strong man, fully armed, guards his castle, his property is safe. [22]But when one stronger than he attacks him and overpowers him, he takes away his armor in which he trusted and divides his plunder. [23]Whoever is not with me is against me, and whoever does not gather with me scatters.

The Return of the Unclean Spirit: 11:24-26

[24]"When the unclean spirit has gone out of a person, it wanders through waterless regions looking for a resting place, but not finding any, it says, 'I will return to my house from which I came.' [25]When it comes, it finds it swept and put in order. [26]Then it goes and brings seven other spirits more evil than itself, and they enter and live there; and the last state of that person is worse than the first."

True Blessedness in Hearing and Obeying It: 11:27-28

[27]While he was saying this, a woman in the crowd raised her voice and said to him, "Blessed is the womb that bore you and the breasts that nursed you!" [28]But he said, "Blessed rather are those who hear the word of God and obey it!"

The Sign of Jonah: 11:29-32

[29]When the crowds were increasing, he began to say, "This generation is an evil generation; it asks for a sign, but no sign will be given to it except the sign of Jonah. [30]For just as Jonah became a sign to the people of Nineveh, so the Son of Man

g   Gk *sons*

will be to this generation. ³¹The queen of the South will rise at the judgment with the people of this generation and condemn them, because she came from the ends of the earth to listen to the wisdom of Solomon, and see, something greater than Solomon is here! ³²The people of Nineveh will rise up at the judgment with this generation and condemn it, because they repented at the proclamation of Jonah, and see, something greater than Jonah is here!

The crowds are fascinated by Jesus. He stirs their expectations of a messiah who will save them. They cannot be sure, however, if he is the one. They want a sign that he is the messiah. They want God to enter their lives, but they want God to enter on their own terms. Jesus repudiates this "evil generation."

He [Jesus] began to say, "This generation is an evil generation; it asks for a sign, but no sign will be given to it except the sign of Jonah. For just as Jonah became a sign to the people of Nineveh, so the Son of Man will be to this generation." 11:29-30

Meditation: The only sign that Jesus offers is the call to repentance and the gift of mercy for those who turn to God. The messianic change that people expect begins with them, their conversion of heart and their acceptance of God's mercy.

Question: How has the sign of Jonah, the call to repentance and to embrace the mercy of God, become evident in my life? Is there a special moment when I heard that call in an especially forceful way?

Let us pray: When we begin to look for signs in our lives, let us remember, Lord, to ask ourselves, "How must we repent, how must we change, and how must we turn?" May we draw courage to face our own call to repentance by the assurance of your mercy that waits to be poured out abundantly upon us.

Putting a Light on a Lampstand: 11:33-36

[33]"No one after lighting a lamp puts it in a cellar,[h] but on the lampstand so that those who enter may see the light. [34]Your eye is the lamp of your body. If your eye is healthy, your whole body is full of light; but if it is not healthy, your body is full of darkness. [35]Therefore consider whether the light in you is not darkness. [36]If then your whole body is full of light, with no part of it in darkness, it will be as full of light as when a lamp gives you light with its rays."

Jesus Renounces the Pharisees and Lawyers and Warns Against Hypocrisy: 11:37-54; 12:1-3

[37]While he was speaking, a Pharisee invited him to dine with him; so he went in and took his place at the table. [38]The Pharisee was amazed to see that he did not first wash before dinner. [39]Then the Lord said to him, "Now you Pharisees clean the outside of the cup and of the dish, but inside you are full of greed and wickedness. [40]You fools! Did not the one who made the outside make the inside also? [41]So give for alms those things that are within; and see, everything will be clean for you.

[42]"But woe to you Pharisees! For you tithe mint and rue and herbs of all kinds, and neglect justice and the love of God; it is these you ought to have practiced, without neglecting the others. [43]Woe to you Pharisees! For you love to have the seat of honor in the synagogues and to be greeted with respect in the marketplaces. [44]Woe to you! For you are like unmarked graves, and people walk over them without realizing it."

[45]One of the lawyers answered him, "Teacher, when you say these things, you insult us too." [46]And he said, "Woe also to you lawyers! For you load people with burdens hard to bear, and you yourselves do not lift a finger to ease them. [47]Woe to you! For you build the tombs of the prophets whom your ancestors killed. [48]So you are witnesses and approve of the deeds of your ancestors; for they killed them, and you build their tombs. [49]Therefore also the Wisdom of God said, 'I will

h   Other ancient authorities add *or under the bushel basket*

send them prophets and apostles, some of whom they will kill and persecute,' ⁵⁰so that this generation may be charged with the blood of all the prophets shed since the foundation of the world, ⁵¹from the blood of Abel to the blood of Zechariah, who perished between the altar and the sanctuary. Yes, I tell you, it will be charged against this generation. ⁵²Woe to you lawyers! For you have taken away the key of knowledge; you did not enter yourselves, and you hindered those who were entering."

⁵³When he went outside, the scribes and the Pharisees began to be very hostile toward him and to cross-examine him about many things, ⁵⁴lying in wait for him, to catch him in something he might say.

Luke 12

A Warning Against Hypocrisy: 12:1-3

[1]Meanwhile, when the crowd gathered by the thousands, so that they trampled on one another, he began to speak first to his disciples, "Beware of the yeast of the Pharisees, that is, their hypocrisy. [2]Nothing is covered up that will not be uncovered, and nothing secret that will not become known. [3]Therefore whatever you have said in the dark will be heard in the light, and what you have whispered behind closed doors will be proclaimed from the housetops.

Depend on God's Merciful Providence to Keep and Protect You, Not on Your Own Designs: 12:4-34

[4]"I tell you, my friends, do not fear those who kill the body, and after that can do nothing more. [5]But I will warn you whom to fear: fear him who, after he has killed, has authority[a] to cast into hell.[b] Yes, I tell you, fear him! [6]Are not five sparrows sold for two pennies? Yet not one of them is forgotten in God's sight. [7]But even the hairs of your head are all counted. Do not be afraid; you are of more value than many sparrows.

[8]"And I tell you, everyone who acknowledges me before others, the Son of Man also will acknowledge before the angels of God; [9]but whoever denies me before others will be denied before the angels of God. [10]And everyone who speaks a word against the Son of Man will be forgiven; but whoever blasphemes against the Holy Spirit will not be forgiven. [11]When they bring you before the synagogues, the rulers, and the authorities, do not worry about how[c] you are to defend yourselves or what you are to say; [12]for the Holy Spirit will teach you at that very hour what you ought to say."

[13]Someone in the crowd said to him, "Teacher, tell my brother to divide the family inheritance with me." [14]But he said to

a   Or *power*
b   Gk *Gehenna*
c   Other ancient authorities add *or what*

him, "Friend, who set me to be a judge or arbitrator over you?"
¹⁵And he said to them, "Take care! Be on your guard against
all kinds of greed; for one's life does not consist in the abundance of possessions." ¹⁶Then he told them a parable: "The
land of a rich man produced abundantly. ¹⁷And he thought
to himself, 'What should I do, for I have no place to store
my crops?' ¹⁸Then he said, 'I will do this: I will pull down my
barns and build larger ones, and there I will store all my grain
and my goods. ¹⁹And I will say to my soul, Soul, you have am-
ple goods laid up for many years; relax, eat, drink, be merry.'
²⁰But God said to him, 'You fool! This very night your life is
being demanded of you. And the things you have prepared,
whose will they be?' ²¹So it is with those who store up trea-
sures for themselves but are not rich toward God."

²²He said to his disciples, "Therefore I tell you, do not worry
about your life, what you will eat, or about your body, what
you will wear. ²³For life is more than food, and the body more
than clothing. ²⁴Consider the ravens: they neither sow nor
reap, they have neither storehouse nor barn, and yet God
feeds them. Of how much more value are you than the birds!
²⁵And can any of you by worrying add a single hour to your
span of life?ᵈ ²⁶If then you are not able to do so small a thing
as that, why do you worry about the rest? ²⁷Consider the
lilies, how they grow: they neither toil nor spin;ᵉ yet I tell
you, even Solomon in all his glory was not clothed like one
of these. ²⁸But if God so clothes the grass of the field, which
is alive today and tomorrow is thrown into the oven, how
much more will he clothe you—you of little faith! ²⁹And do
not keep striving for what you are to eat and what you are to
drink, and do not keep worrying. ³⁰For it is the nations of the
world that strive after all these things, and your Father knows
that you need them. ³¹Instead, strive for hisᶠ kingdom, and
these things will be given to you as well.

³²"Do not be afraid, little flock, for it is your Father's good
pleasure to give you the kingdom. ³³Sell your possessions,
and give alms. Make purses for yourselves that do not wear
out, an unfailing treasure in heaven, where no thief comes

d   Or *add a cubit to your stature*
e   Other ancient authorities read *Consider the lilies; they neither spin nor weave*
f   Other ancient authorities read *God's*

near and no moth destroys. [34]For where your treasure is, there your heart will be also.

Be Attentive and Alert to the Master's Arrival: 12:35-48

[35]"Be dressed for action and have your lamps lit; [36]be like those who are waiting for their master to return from the wedding banquet, so that they may open the door for him as soon as he comes and knocks. [37]Blessed are those slaves whom the master finds alert when he comes; truly I tell you, he will fasten his belt and have them sit down to eat, and he will come and serve them. [38]If he comes during the middle of the night, or near dawn, and finds them so, blessed are those slaves.

[39]"But know this: if the owner of the house had known at what hour the thief was coming, he[g] would not have let his house be broken into. [40]You also must be ready, for the Son of Man is coming at an unexpected hour."

[41]Peter said, "Lord, are you telling this parable for us or for everyone?" [42]And the Lord said, "Who then is the faithful and prudent manager whom his master will put in charge of his slaves, to give them their allowance of food at the proper time? [43]Blessed is that slave whom his master will find at work when he arrives. [44]Truly I tell you, he will put that one in charge of all his possessions. [45]But if that slave says to himself, 'My master is delayed in coming,' and if he begins to beat the other slaves, men and women, and to eat and drink and get drunk, [46]the master of that slave will come on a day when he does not expect him and at an hour that he does not know, and will cut him in pieces,[h] and put him with the unfaithful. [47]That slave who knew what his master wanted, but did not prepare himself or do what was wanted, will receive a severe beating. [48]But the one who did not know and did what deserved a beating will receive a light beating. From everyone to whom much has been given, much will be required; and from the one to whom much has been entrusted, even more will be demanded.

g   Other ancient authorities add *would have watched and*
h   Or *cut him off*

Jesus Calls to Decision and so Causes Divisions: 12:49-53

[49]"I came to bring fire to the earth, and how I wish it were already kindled! [50]I have a baptism with which to be baptized, and what stress I am under until it is completed! [51]Do you think that I have come to bring peace to the earth? No, I tell you, but rather division! [52]From now on five in one household will be divided, three against two and two against three; [53]they will be divided: father against son and son against father, mother against daughter and daughter against mother, mother-in-law against her daughter-in-law and daughter-in-law against mother-in-law."

The Urgency of Interpreting the Signs of the Times and Settling with Opponents: 12:54-59

[54]He also said to the crowds, "When you see a cloud rising in the west, you immediately say, 'It is going to rain'; and so it happens. [55]And when you see the south wind blowing, you say, 'There will be scorching heat'; and it happens. [56]You hypocrites! You know how to interpret the appearance of earth and sky, but why do you not know how to interpret the present time?

[57]"And why do you not judge for yourselves what is right? [58]Thus, when you go with your accuser before a magistrate, on the way make an effort to settle the case,[i] or you may be dragged before the judge, and the judge hand you over to the officer, and the officer throw you in prison. [59]I tell you, you will never get out until you have paid the very last penny."

---

i   Gk *settle with him*

Luke 13

The Need and Urgency of Repentance: 13:1-9

> [1]At that very time there were some present who told him about the Galileans whose blood Pilate had mingled with their sacrifices. [2]He asked them, "Do you think that because these Galileans suffered in this way they were worse sinners than all other Galileans? [3]No, I tell you; but unless you repent, you will all perish as they did. [4]Or those eighteen who were killed when the tower of Siloam fell on them—do you think that they were worse offenders than all the others living in Jerusalem? [5]No, I tell you; but unless you repent, you will all perish just as they did."
>
> [6]Then he told this parable: "A man had a fig tree planted in his vineyard; and he came looking for fruit on it and found none. [7]So he said to the gardener, 'See here! For three years I have come looking for fruit on this fig tree, and still I find none. Cut it down! Why should it be wasting the soil?' [8]He replied, 'Sir, let it alone for one more year, until I dig around it and put manure on it. [9]If it bears fruit next year, well and good; but if not, you can cut it down.'"

When Jesus speaks of the Galileans whom Pilate slaughtered, of those who died when the tower at Siloam collapsed on them, and of the barren fig tree, he imparts an important message about the urgency of repentance to obtain mercy.

Of the Galileans who perished at Pilate's hands: *"unless you repent, you will all perish as they did."* 13:3

Of those who died at the tower of Siloam: *"unless you repent, you will all perish just as they did."* 13:5

Of the barren fig tree: *"If it bears fruit next year, well and good; but if not, you can cut it down."* 13:9

Meditation: The mercy of God is never imposed upon us, never forced upon us. The mercy of God, which is sheer grace, takes hold of our lives when we repent and turn to the Lord. If we want mercy, we cooperate with the grace of God and commit ourselves to repentance.

Question: Is turning to the mercy of God an urgent matter for me? Are there other things that seem to outstrip it as a priority?

> **Let us pray:** Let us never delay turning to you, O Lord. When we sincerely embrace a path of conversion and repentance, we are sure of your mercy taking hold of us and bringing us to new life.

Jesus Heals a Crippled Woman on the Sabbath: 13:10-17

[10]Now he was teaching in one of the synagogues on the sabbath. [11]And just then there appeared a woman with a spirit that had crippled her for eighteen years. She was bent over and was quite unable to stand up straight. [12]When Jesus saw her, he called her over and said, "Woman, you are set free from your ailment." [13]When he laid his hands on her, immediately she stood up straight and began praising God. [14]But the leader of the synagogue, indignant because Jesus had cured on the sabbath, kept saying to the crowd, "There are six days on which work ought to be done; come on those days and be cured, and not on the sabbath day." [15]But the Lord answered him and said, "You hypocrites! Does not each of you on the sabbath untie his ox or his donkey from the manger, and lead it away to give it water? [16]And ought not this woman, a daughter of Abraham whom Satan bound for eighteen long years, be set free from this bondage on the sabbath day?" [17]When he said this, all his opponents were put to shame; and the entire crowd was rejoicing at all the wonderful things that he was doing.

Jesus is moved to act by the logic of compassion and mercy, not the logic of law. By healing a crippled woman on the Sabbath and in a synagogue, he incurs the wrath of the religious leaders who are crippled by a blind and inconsistent application of religious law. In his mercy, Jesus moves freely to free others.

"And ought not this woman, a daughter of Abraham whom Satan bound for eighteen long years, be set free from this bondage on the sabbath day?" 13:6

Meditation: The mercy of God frees us to be the persons who God wants us to be—whole, healthy, and joyful. The distortions of sin and sickness that bind us come undone when the mercy of God touches our lives. We become free in the truest sense of the word.

Question: Although I do not want to be like the religious leaders in the gospel who are wrapped up in their own self-righteousness, how do I ensure that does not happen? How can I avoid the trap of self?

Let us pray: In your great mercy, O Lord, free us from all that binds us. Let us rejoice in your compassion that heals and sustains us and makes us as you meant us to be—your beloved daughters and sons.

Parables of the Kingdom: The Mustard Seed, Yeast at Work, the Narrow Door: 13:18-30

[18]He said therefore, "What is the kingdom of God like? And to what should I compare it? [19]It is like a mustard seed that someone took and sowed in the garden; it grew and became a tree, and the birds of the air made nests in its branches."

[20]And again he said, "To what should I compare the kingdom of God? [21]It is like yeast that a woman took and mixed in with[a] three measures of flour until all of it was leavened."

[22]Jesus[b] went through one town and village after another, teaching as he made his way to Jerusalem. [23]Someone asked

a   Gk *hid in*
b   Gk *He*

him, "Lord, will only a few be saved?" He said to them,
²⁴"Strive to enter through the narrow door; for many, I tell
you, will try to enter and will not be able. ²⁵When once the
owner of the house has got up and shut the door, and you
begin to stand outside and to knock at the door, saying, 'Lord,
open to us,' then in reply he will say to you, 'I do not know
where you come from.' ²⁶Then you will begin to say, 'We ate
and drank with you, and you taught in our streets.' ²⁷But he
will say, 'I do not know where you come from; go away from
me, all you evildoers!' ²⁸There will be weeping and gnashing
of teeth when you see Abraham and Isaac and Jacob and all
the prophets in the kingdom of God, and you yourselves
thrown out. ²⁹Then people will come from east and west,
from north and south, and will eat in the kingdom of God.
³⁰Indeed, some are last who will be first, and some are first
who will be last."

Jesus Laments the Fate of Jerusalem: 13:31-35

³¹At that very hour some Pharisees came and said to him,
"Get away from here, for Herod wants to kill you." ³²He said
to them, "Go and tell that fox for me,ᶜ 'Listen, I am casting
out demons and performing cures today and tomorrow, and
on the third day I finish my work. ³³Yet today, tomorrow, and
the next day I must be on my way, because it is impossible
for a prophet to be killed outside of Jerusalem.' ³⁴Jerusalem,
Jerusalem, the city that kills the prophets and stones those
who are sent to it! How often have I desired to gather your
children together as a hen gathers her brood under her wings,
and you were not willing! ³⁵See, your house is left to you. And
I tell you, you will not see me until the time comes whenᵈ
you say, 'Blessed is the one who comes in the name of the
Lord.'"

c   Gk lacks *for me*
d   Other ancient authorities lack *the time comes when*

Luke 14

Jesus Heals a Man with Dropsy on the Sabbath and Lets Mercy Break Through Legalism: 14:1-6

[1]On one occasion when Jesus[a] was going to the house of a leader of the Pharisees to eat a meal on the sabbath, they were watching him closely. [2]Just then, in front of him, there was a man who had dropsy. [3]And Jesus asked the lawyers and Pharisees, "Is it lawful to cure people on the sabbath, or not?" [4]But they were silent. So Jesus[b] took him and healed him, and sent him away. [5]Then he said to them, "If one of you has a child[c] or an ox that has fallen into a well, will you not immediately pull it out on a sabbath day?" [6]And they could not reply to this.

The Rules of Hospitality in the Merciful Kingdom of God: 14:7-24

[7]When he noticed how the guests chose the places of honor, he told them a parable. [8]"When you are invited by someone to a wedding banquet, do not sit down at the place of honor, in case someone more distinguished than you has been invited by your host; [9]and the host who invited both of you may come and say to you, 'Give this person your place,' and then in disgrace you would start to take the lowest place. [10]But when you are invited, go and sit down at the lowest place, so that when your host comes, he may say to you, 'Friend, move up higher'; then you will be honored in the presence of all who sit at the table with you. [11]For all who exalt themselves will be humbled, and those who humble themselves will be exalted."

[12]He said also to the one who had invited him, "When you give a luncheon or a dinner, do not invite your friends or your brothers or your relatives or rich neighbors, in case they may invite you in return, and you would be repaid. [13]But when you give a banquet, invite the poor, the crippled, the

a   Gk *he*
b   Gk *he*
c   Other ancient authorities read *a donkey*

lame, and the blind. [14]And you will be blessed, because they cannot repay you, for you will be repaid at the resurrection of the righteous."

[15]One of the dinner guests, on hearing this, said to him, "Blessed is anyone who will eat bread in the kingdom of God!" [16]Then Jesus[d] said to him, "Someone gave a great dinner and invited many. [17]At the time for the dinner he sent his slave to say to those who had been invited, 'Come; for everything is ready now.' [18]But they all alike began to make excuses. The first said to him, 'I have bought a piece of land, and I must go out and see it; please accept my regrets.' [19]Another said, 'I have bought five yoke of oxen, and I am going to try them out; please accept my regrets.' [20]Another said, 'I have just been married, and therefore I cannot come.' [21]So the slave returned and reported this to his master. Then the owner of the house became angry and said to his slave, 'Go out at once into the streets and lanes of the town and bring in the poor, the crippled, the blind, and the lame.' [22]And the slave said, 'Sir, what you ordered has been done, and there is still room.' [23]Then the master said to the slave, 'Go out into the roads and lanes, and compel people to come in, so that my house may be filled. [24]For I tell you,[e] none of those who were invited will taste my dinner.'"

In Luke's gospel, meals are often the setting where Jesus teaches or heals. All of these meals with the Lord anticipate the heavenly banquet in the Kingdom of God. Unlike ordinary hospitality, which is often self-serving, these meals reflect values set off from the ordinary. They are marked by divine mercy.

"But when you give a banquet, invite the poor, the crippled, the lame, and the blind. And you will be blessed, because they cannot repay you, for you will be repaid at the resurrection of the righteous." 14:13-14

"Go out at once into the streets and lanes of the town and bring in the poor, the crippled, the blind, and the lame." ... *"Go out into the roads and lanes, and compel people to come in, so that my house may be filled."* 14:21, 23

d   Gk *he*
e   The Greek word for *you* here is plural

Meditation: The mercy of God enables the invitation to the great banquet to be wide and generous. There is no question of restricting the guest list. There are no fine lines of social calculation. The banquet of mercy is generous and stretches wide to embrace as many as possible.

Question: How do my life and circumstances mirror the expansiveness of God's mercy? What do I need to do to make my love less restrictive?

> **Let us pray:** When our narrow spirits want to restrict those whom we will receive into our lives, expand our hearts, O Lord, so that we can genuinely and widely welcome many people into our lives. Give us the blessing of a generous heart that reflects the generosity of your mercy at work in the world.

The Cost of Discipleship is a Complete and Total Commitment: 14:25-33

[25]Now large crowds were traveling with him; and he turned and said to them, [26]"Whoever comes to me and does not hate father and mother, wife and children, brothers and sisters, yes, and even life itself, cannot be my disciple. [27]Whoever does not carry the cross and follow me cannot be my disciple. [28]For which of you, intending to build a tower, does not first sit down and estimate the cost, to see whether he has enough to complete it? [29]Otherwise, when he has laid a foundation and is not able to finish, all who see it will begin to ridicule him, [30]saying, 'This fellow began to build and was not able to finish.' [31]Or what king, going out to wage war against another king, will not sit down first and consider whether he is able with ten thousand to oppose the one who comes against him with twenty thousand? [32]If he cannot, then, while the other is still far away, he sends a delegation and asks for the terms of peace. [33]So therefore, none of you can become my disciple if you do not give up all your possessions.

A Saying About Salt: 14:34-35

[34]"Salt is good; but if salt has lost its taste, how can its salt-iness be restored?[f] [35]It is fit neither for the soil nor for the manure pile; they throw it away. Let anyone with ears to hear listen!"

---

f   Or *how can it be used for seasoning?*

Luke 15

The Parables of the Lost Sheep and the Lost Coin: 15:1-10

[1]Now all the tax collectors and sinners were coming near to listen to him. [2]And the Pharisees and the scribes were grumbling and saying, "This fellow welcomes sinners and eats with them."

[3]So he told them this parable: [4]"Which one of you, having a hundred sheep and losing one of them, does not leave the ninety-nine in the wilderness and go after the one that is lost until he finds it? [5]When he has found it, he lays it on his shoulders and rejoices. [6]And when he comes home, he calls together his friends and neighbors, saying to them, 'Rejoice with me, for I have found my sheep that was lost.' [7]Just so, I tell you, there will be more joy in heaven over one sinner who repents than over ninety-nine righteous persons who need no repentance.

[8]"Or what woman having ten silver coins,[a] if she loses one of them, does not light a lamp, sweep the house, and search carefully until she finds it? [9]When she has found it, she calls together her friends and neighbors, saying, 'Rejoice with me, for I have found the coin that I had lost.' [10]Just so, I tell you, there is joy in the presence of the angels of God over one sinner who repents."

A shepherd tirelessly pursues one lost sheep until he finds it. A woman diligently sweeps her house until she finds the coin she has lost. Before we pursue the mercy of God, the mercy of God pursues us.

"And when he comes home, he calls together his friends and neighbors, saying to them, 'Rejoice with me, for I have found my sheep that was lost.' Just so, I tell you, there will be more joy in heaven over one sinner who repents than over ninety-nine righteous persons who need no repentance." 15:6-7

---

a   Gk *drachmas*, each worth about a day's wage for a laborer

"When she has found it, she calls together her friends and neighbors, saying, 'Rejoice with me, for I have found the coin that I had lost.'" 15:9

Meditation: The mercy of God does, indeed, relentlessly pursue us. When we are found, when we have accepted that mercy, God rejoices. A phrase in the Psalms says, "The Lord takes pleasure in his people." (Ps 149:4) Amazingly, God does not so much rejoice because we are good and have done good things, but because we have turned to him and embraced his loving mercy that brings us home.

Question: What would it look like, if we were to search diligently, as the God of mercy does, for those who have lost their way? Would I do something like that?

Let us pray: O God, ever faithful and true, may you forever celebrate our return to you. And may you hold us up for all to see as the great works of your mercy—those who were lost but now are found.

The Parable of the Loving Father, the Prodigal Son, and the Elder Brother: 15:11-32

[11]Then Jesus[b] said, "There was a man who had two sons. [12]The younger of them said to his father, 'Father, give me the share of the property that will belong to me.' So he divided his property between them. [13]A few days later the younger son gathered all he had and traveled to a distant country, and there he squandered his property in dissolute living. [14]When he had spent everything, a severe famine took place throughout that country, and he began to be in need. [15]So he went and hired himself out to one of the citizens of that country, who sent him to his fields to feed the pigs. [16]He would gladly have filled himself with[c] the pods that the pigs were eating; and no one gave him anything. [17]But when he came to himself he said, 'How many of my father's hired hands have bread enough and to spare, but here I am dying

b   Gk *he*
c   Other ancient authorities read *filled his stomach with*

of hunger! [18]I will get up and go to my father, and I will say to him, "Father, I have sinned against heaven and before you; [19]I am no longer worthy to be called your son; treat me like one of your hired hands.'" [20]So he set off and went to his father. But while he was still far off, his father saw him and was filled with compassion; he ran and put his arms around him and kissed him. [21]Then the son said to him, 'Father, I have sinned against heaven and before you; I am no longer worthy to be called your son.'[d] [22]But the father said to his slaves, 'Quickly, bring out a robe—the best one—and put it on him; put a ring on his finger and sandals on his feet. [23]And get the fatted calf and kill it, and let us eat and celebrate; [24]for this son of mine was dead and is alive again; he was lost and is found!' And they began to celebrate.

[25]"Now his elder son was in the field; and when he came and approached the house, he heard music and dancing. [26]He called one of the slaves and asked what was going on. [27]He replied, 'Your brother has come, and your father has killed the fatted calf, because he has got him back safe and sound.' [28]Then he became angry and refused to go in. His father came out and began to plead with him. [29]But he answered his father, 'Listen! For all these years I have been working like a slave for you, and I have never disobeyed your command; yet you have never given me even a young goat so that I might celebrate with my friends. [30]But when this son of yours came back, who has devoured your property with prostitutes, you killed the fatted calf for him!' [31]Then the father[e] said to him, 'Son, you are always with me, and all that is mine is yours. [32]But we had to celebrate and rejoice, because this brother of yours was dead and has come to life; he was lost and has been found.'"

The story of the loving father, the prodigal son, and the elder son is unique to Luke. This parable reveals God's intent for us, especially when we have gone astray. In describing the attitudes of the two sons with all their limitations and sinfulness, Jesus underscores the undaunted mercy of God that embraces both men and draws them close to himself.

"…here I am dying of hunger! I will get up and go to my father, and I will say to him, 'Father, I have sinned against heaven and before you…' his father saw him and was filled with compassion; he ran and put his arms around him and kissed him." 15:17-18, 20

"Then he [the elder son] became angry and refused to go in. His father came out and began to plead with him…Then the father said to him,'… we had to celebrate and rejoice, because this brother of yours was dead and has come to life; he was lost and has been found.'" 15:28, 31-32

Meditation: The younger son's motivation to go home stems fundamentally from his hunger and lack of resources. You can wonder how sincere his confession is—*Father, I have sinned against heaven and before you*. The depth of his contrition, however, does not matter as much as the father's mercy and compassion, as he runs out to meet him. Similarly, the elder son's resentment does not matter as much as the father's concern that leads him to go outside and plead with his son. The amazing readiness of God's mercy assures us that our mixed motivations and our own less-than-ideal contrition can in no way thwart God's mercy in our lives.

Question: When God deals with us in his mercy, he also deals with all our limitations. How do we deal with the limitations of others, especially in those moments when we are trying to do good for them and they may not be especially responsive?

Let us pray: Bring us to sincere repentance, O Lord, so that we can turn to you and your mercy. When our own self-centeredness or our resentments threaten to subvert your forgiveness, run to us, plead with us, and embrace us with your love, which is greater than our hearts.

Luke 16

The Parable of the Dishonest Manager: 16:1-13

[1]Then Jesus[a] said to the disciples, "There was a rich man who had a manager, and charges were brought to him that this man was squandering his property. [2]So he summoned him and said to him, 'What is this that I hear about you? Give me an accounting of your management, because you cannot be my manager any longer.' [3]Then the manager said to himself, 'What will I do, now that my master is taking the position away from me? I am not strong enough to dig, and I am ashamed to beg. [4]I have decided what to do so that, when I am dismissed as manager, people may welcome me into their homes.' [5]So, summoning his master's debtors one by one, he asked the first, 'How much do you owe my master?' [6]He answered, 'A hundred jugs of olive oil.' He said to him, 'Take your bill, sit down quickly, and make it fifty.' [7]Then he asked another, 'And how much do you owe?' He replied, 'A hundred containers of wheat.' He said to him, 'Take your bill and make it eighty.' [8]And his master commended the dishonest manager because he had acted shrewdly; for the children of this age are more shrewd in dealing with their own generation than are the children of light. [9]And I tell you, make friends for yourselves by means of dishonest wealth[b] so that when it is gone, they may welcome you into the eternal homes.[c]

[10]"Whoever is faithful in a very little is faithful also in much; and whoever is dishonest in a very little is dishonest also in much. [11]If then you have not been faithful with the dishonest wealth,[d] who will entrust to you the true riches? [12]And if you have not been faithful with what belongs to another, who will give you what is your own? [13]No slave can serve two masters; for a slave will either hate the one and love the other, or be devoted to the one and despise the other. You cannot serve God and wealth."[e]

---

a   Gk *he*
b   Gk *mammon*
c   Gk *tents*
d   Gk *mammon*
e   Gk *mammon*

The Law and the Kingdom of God: 16:14-18

[14]The Pharisees, who were lovers of money, heard all this, and they ridiculed him. [15]So he said to them, "You are those who justify yourselves in the sight of others; but God knows your hearts; for what is prized by human beings is an abomination in the sight of God.

[16]"The law and the prophets were in effect until John came; since then the good news of the kingdom of God is proclaimed, and everyone tries to enter it by force.[f] [17]But it is easier for heaven and earth to pass away, than for one stroke of a letter in the law to be dropped.

[18]"Anyone who divorces his wife and marries another commits adultery, and whoever marries a woman divorced from her husband commits adultery.

The Rich Man and Lazarus: 16:19-31

[19]"There was a rich man who was dressed in purple and fine linen and who feasted sumptuously every day. [20]And at his gate lay a poor man named Lazarus, covered with sores, [21]who longed to satisfy his hunger with what fell from the rich man's table; even the dogs would come and lick his sores. [22]The poor man died and was carried away by the angels to be with Abraham.[g] The rich man also died and was buried. [23]In Hades, where he was being tormented, he looked up and saw Abraham far away with Lazarus by his side.[h] [24]He called out, 'Father Abraham, have mercy on me, and send Lazarus to dip the tip of his finger in water and cool my tongue; for I am in agony in these flames.' [25]But Abraham said, 'Child, remember that during your lifetime you received your good things, and Lazarus in like manner evil things; but now he is comforted here, and you are in agony. [26]Besides all this, between you and us a great chasm has been fixed, so that those who might want to pass from here to you cannot do so, and no one can cross from there to us.' [27]He said, 'Then, father, I beg you to send him to my father's house—[28]for I have five

f   Or *everyone is strongly urged to enter it*
g   Gk *to Abraham's bosom*
h   Gk *in his bosom*

brothers—that he may warn them, so that they will not also come into this place of torment.' [29]Abraham replied, 'They have Moses and the prophets; they should listen to them.' [30]He said, 'No, father Abraham; but if someone goes to them from the dead, they will repent.' [31]He said to him, 'If they do not listen to Moses and the prophets, neither will they be convinced even if someone rises from the dead.'"

The story of the rich man who dines sumptuously and the starving beggar Lazarus who is positioned outside his door teaches us two lessons about mercy. First, God's mercy triumphs when the Lord receives Lazarus into the heavenly banquet. Second, our lack of mercy, which can shut us out of the heavenly banquet, probably does not so much stem from our being unmerciful or cruel but rather from being oblivious and, therefore, indifferent to those who are close by— outside our door—and who are in deep or dire need of our help.

"There was a rich man who was dressed in purple and fine linen and who feasted sumptuously every day. And at his gate lay a poor man named Lazarus, covered with sores, who longed to satisfy his hunger..." 16:19-21

Meditation: The rich man does nothing evil against Lazarus, the poor man who needs his mercy. To the rich man who is absorbed in his own pleasures and satisfactions, Lazarus, seated on the other side of the gate, is invisible. Before we act with mercy, we must notice. We must be attentive. Otherwise we will be, like the rich man, lost in ourselves and indifferent to what and who lies outside the door. Our mercy begins with our attention.

Question: How can I train myself to be attentive and to notice the people and the needs of those around me?

Let us pray: Merciful God, you look on your people with compassion. You always notice their need and you are aware of all their struggles. Give us the capacity to see the needs of those we meet and of those who might be shielded from our view. In this way, we will be always ready to be compassionate and merciful.

Luke 17

Some Sayings of Jesus: 17:1-10

[1]Jesus[a] said to his disciples, "Occasions for stumbling are bound to come, but woe to anyone by whom they come! [2]It would be better for you if a millstone were hung around your neck and you were thrown into the sea than for you to cause one of these little ones to stumble. [3]Be on your guard! If another disciple[b] sins, you must rebuke the offender, and if there is repentance, you must forgive. [4]And if the same person sins against you seven times a day, and turns back to you seven times and says, 'I repent,' you must forgive."

[5]The apostles said to the Lord, "Increase our faith!" [6]The Lord replied, "If you had faith the size of a[c] mustard seed, you could say to this mulberry tree, 'Be uprooted and planted in the sea,' and it would obey you.

[7]"Who among you would say to your slave who has just come in from plowing or tending sheep in the field, 'Come here at once and take your place at the table'? [8]Would you not rather say to him, 'Prepare supper for me, put on your apron and serve me while I eat and drink; later you may eat and drink'? [9]Do you thank the slave for doing what was commanded? [10]So you also, when you have done all that you were ordered to do, say, 'We are worthless slaves; we have done only what we ought to have done!'"

Among the sayings of Jesus are directions for forgiving those who offend us. If we are merciful as our heavenly Father is merciful, then, Jesus says, we follow the patterns of divine forgiveness. That forgiveness comes not just once but over and over again.

"Be on your guard! If another disciple sins, you must rebuke the offender, and if there is repentance, you must forgive. And if the same person sins against you seven times a day, and turns back to you seven times and says, 'I repent,' you must forgive." 17:3-4

a   Gk *He*
b   Gk *your brother*
c   Gk *faith as a grain of*

Meditation: The mercy of God is never exhausted. Our willingness to extend mercy through forgiveness cannot be limited. Naturally, human beings tire, especially when they are offended over and over again. For those who believe, God's mercy is at work within them, and that mercy is never exhausted.

Question: What resources do I need to be patient and merciful with people who continue to offend me over and over again?

> **Let us pray:** Give us, O Lord, the grace of persevering mercy that never tires. Let your mercy work through us for the forgiveness of our brothers and sisters—without hesitation and without measure.

Jesus Cleanses Ten Lepers: 17:11-19

[11]On the way to Jerusalem Jesus[d] was going through the region between Samaria and Galilee. [12]As he entered a village, ten lepers[e] approached him. Keeping their distance, [13]they called out, saying, "Jesus, Master, have mercy on us!" [14]When he saw them, he said to them, "Go and show yourselves to the priests." And as they went, they were made clean. [15]Then one of them, when he saw that he was healed, turned back, praising God with a loud voice. [16]He prostrated himself at Jesus'[f] feet and thanked him. And he was a Samaritan. [17]Then Jesus asked, "Were not ten made clean? But the other nine, where are they? [18]Was none of them found to return and give praise to God except this foreigner?" [19]Then he said to him, "Get up and go on your way; your faith has made you well."

Jesus looked mercifully upon the lepers he met. He knew their physical suffering and social isolation. He also understood how they might interpret their illness as a sign of God's displeasure with them. Jesus healed them, re-integrated them into their communities, and

d   Gk *he*
e   The terms *leper* and *leprosy* can refer to several diseases
f   Gk *his*

let them know that they had God's favor. In this story of healing, only one grateful person benefits fully from Jesus' compassion, because his gratitude is a confession of faith. That grateful faith enables him to receive God's mercy in full measure.

When he saw them, he said to them, "Go and show yourselves to the priests." And as they went, they were made clean. Then one of them, when he saw that he was healed, turned back, praising God with a loud voice. He…thanked him…Then he said to him, "Get up and go on your way; your faith has made you well." 17:14-15, 19

Meditation: God's mercy means little if it is offered but not accepted. It is never, of course, imposed upon us. The sure sign of freely accepting God's mercy is our gratitude. In thanksgiving, we acknowledge that we have received something that is not merited, earned, or deserved. In thanksgiving, we allow God's mercy to fully take hold of us. That is why Jesus says to the man, *"Your faith has made you well."* He was already well in some sense, but this man's thanksgiving brought him to that integral and complete wellness that is only possible with faith.

Question: When I consider the prayers I offer to the Lord, how and how often do I offer prayers of gratitude to God for his mercy and gifts to me?

Let us pray: With the Psalmist, I pray, "Forever I will sing the mercies of the Lord." Forever, O Lord, may I be mindful of my indebtedness to your mercy. Let me praise your goodness and thank you always. Then your healing mercy will completely envelop me.

The Kingdom of God Comes in its Own Time and on its Own Terms: 17:20-37

[20]Once Jesus[g] was asked by the Pharisees when the kingdom of God was coming, and he answered, "The kingdom of God

g   Gk *he*

is not coming with things that can be observed; ²¹nor will they say, 'Look, here it is!' or 'There it is!' For, in fact, the kingdom of God is among[h] you."

²²Then he said to the disciples, "The days are coming when you will long to see one of the days of the Son of Man, and you will not see it. ²³They will say to you, 'Look there!' or 'Look here!' Do not go, do not set off in pursuit. ²⁴For as the lightning flashes and lights up the sky from one side to the other, so will the Son of Man be in his day.[i] ²⁵But first he must endure much suffering and be rejected by this generation. ²⁶Just as it was in the days of Noah, so too it will be in the days of the Son of Man. ²⁷They were eating and drinking, and marrying and being given in marriage, until the day Noah entered the ark, and the flood came and destroyed all of them. ²⁸Likewise, just as it was in the days of Lot: they were eating and drinking, buying and selling, planting and building, ²⁹but on the day that Lot left Sodom, it rained fire and sulfur from heaven and destroyed all of them ³⁰—it will be like that on the day that the Son of Man is revealed. ³¹On that day, anyone on the housetop who has belongings in the house must not come down to take them away; and likewise anyone in the field must not turn back. ³²Remember Lot's wife. ³³Those who try to make their life secure will lose it, but those who lose their life will keep it. ³⁴I tell you, on that night there will be two in one bed; one will be taken and the other left. ³⁵There will be two women grinding meal together; one will be taken and the other left."[j] ³⁷Then they asked him, "Where, Lord?" He said to them, "Where the corpse is, there the vultures will gather."

---

h   Or *within*
i   Other ancient authorities lack *in his day*
j   Other ancient authorities add verse 36, *"Two will be in the field; one will be taken and the other left."*

Luke 18

Perseverance in Prayer, the Parable of the Widow and the Unjust Judge: 18:1-8

[1]Then Jesus[a] told them a parable about their need to pray always and not to lose heart. [2]He said, "In a certain city there was a judge who neither feared God nor had respect for people. [3]In that city there was a widow who kept coming to him and saying, 'Grant me justice against my opponent.' [4]For a while he refused; but later he said to himself, 'Though I have no fear of God and no respect for anyone, [5]yet because this widow keeps bothering me, I will grant her justice, so that she may not wear me out by continually coming.'"[b] [6]And the Lord said, "Listen to what the unjust judge says. [7]And will not God grant justice to his chosen ones who cry to him day and night? Will he delay long in helping them? [8]I tell you, he will quickly grant justice to them. And yet, when the Son of Man comes, will he find faith on earth?"

The Parable of the Pharisee and the Tax Collector: 18:9-14

[9]He also told this parable to some who trusted in themselves that they were righteous and regarded others with contempt: [10]"Two men went up to the temple to pray, one a Pharisee and the other a tax collector. [11]The Pharisee, standing by himself, was praying thus, 'God, I thank you that I am not like other people: thieves, rogues, adulterers, or even like this tax collector. [12]I fast twice a week; I give a tenth of all my income.' [13]But the tax collector, standing far off, would not even look up to heaven, but was beating his breast and saying, 'God, be merciful to me, a sinner!' [14]I tell you, this man went down to his home justified rather than the other; for all who exalt themselves will be humbled, but all who humble themselves will be exalted."

To receive God's mercy really and truly into our lives means that we not compare ourselves with others but take ourselves as we are. It also

a   Gk *he*
b   Or *so that she may not finally come and slap me in the face*

means that we set aside any sense of self-sufficiency and acknowledge our complete reliance upon God's mercy.

"The Pharisee…was praying thus, 'God, I thank you that I am not like other people…'" 18:11

"The tax collector…was beating his breast and saying, 'God, be merciful to me a sinner!' I tell you, this man went down to his home justified rather than the other…" 18:13-14

Meditation: How we go before God makes all the difference for encountering God's mercy. In this story, two men take entirely different approaches to the Lord. The Pharisee does not so much pray to God as praise himself. We are likely not to be so blatant, but we can easily share in his sense of self-satisfaction. The tax collector, on the other hand, knows his need, focuses on the mercy of God, and surrenders to him. He goes home touched and transformed by the mercy of God.

Question: Do I compare myself spiritually to others? Has this caused me to not appreciate God's merciful gifts in my life? Do I generally find myself better than others or generally find myself worse than others?

Let us pray: Let us never fear, O Lord, to see ourselves as we are. Let us never fear to come before you just as we are. And when we stand before you, let us not be absorbed by ourselves and either the good or the evil that we have done, but be focused on you alone, the source of mercy and hope.

Jesus Blesses Little Children: 18:15-17

[15]People were bringing even infants to him that he might touch them; and when the disciples saw it, they sternly ordered them not to do it. [16]But Jesus called for them and said, "Let the little children come to me, and do not stop them; for

it is to such as these that the kingdom of God belongs. ¹⁷Truly I tell you, whoever does not receive the kingdom of God as a little child will never enter it."

The Rich Ruler Seeks to Inherit Eternal Life: 18:18-30

¹⁸A certain ruler asked him, "Good Teacher, what must I do to inherit eternal life?" ¹⁹Jesus said to him, "Why do you call me good? No one is good but God alone. ²⁰You know the commandments: 'You shall not commit adultery; You shall not murder; You shall not steal; You shall not bear false witness; Honor your father and mother.'" ²¹He replied, "I have kept all these since my youth." ²²When Jesus heard this, he said to him, "There is still one thing lacking. Sell all that you own and distribute the moneyᶜ to the poor, and you will have treasure in heaven; then come, follow me." ²³But when he heard this, he became sad; for he was very rich. ²⁴Jesus looked at him and said, "How hard it is for those who have wealth to enter the kingdom of God! ²⁵Indeed, it is easier for a camel to go through the eye of a needle than for someone who is rich to enter the kingdom of God."

²⁶Those who heard it said, "Then who can be saved?" ²⁷He replied, "What is impossible for mortals is possible for God."

²⁸Then Peter said, "Look, we have left our homes and followed you." ²⁹And he said to them, "Truly I tell you, there is no one who has left house or wife or brothers or parents or children, for the sake of the kingdom of God, ³⁰who will not get back very much more in this age, and in the age to come eternal life."

Jesus meets a rich man who wants to know what he should do to inherit eternal life. Jesus reviews the commandments, and the man affirms that he has kept them. Then Jesus invites him to take another step, to sell what he has, give it to the poor, and follow Jesus. The rich man is unable to take that step, and he is sad.

He replied, "I have kept all these [commandments] since my youth." When Jesus heard this, he said to him, "There is still one thing lacking. Sell all

c   Gk lacks *the money*

that you own and distribute the money to the poor…then come, follow me." 18:21-22

> **Meditation**: The path that leads to eternal life, Jesus says, includes observing the commandments—doing what is right and good and avoiding evil. More, however, is required. The rich ruler is called not only to live righteously by observing the commandments but also to live mercifully and compassionately by caring for the poor. Following Jesus is not only a matter of rectitude but of compassionate mercy.
>
> **Question:** Am I firmly locked into my own idea of what it means to follow Jesus? Is there flexibility within me to hear his voice and to move in a new and unexpected direction?
>
> **Let us pray:** Open our hearts, O Lord, to walk in the steps of Jesus, so that we will not be satisfied only in doing what is right but will always strive to do what is loving and merciful.

Jesus Foretells His Death and Resurrection a Third Time: 18:31-34

[31]Then he took the twelve aside and said to them, "See, we are going up to Jerusalem, and everything that is written about the Son of Man by the prophets will be accomplished. [32]For he will be handed over to the Gentiles; and he will be mocked and insulted and spat upon. [33]After they have flogged him, they will kill him, and on the third day he will rise again." [34]But they understood nothing about all these things; in fact, what he said was hidden from them, and they did not grasp what was said.

Jesus Heals a Blind Beggar Near Jericho: 18:35-43

[35]As he approached Jericho, a blind man was sitting by the roadside begging. [36]When he heard a crowd going by, he asked what was happening. [37]They told him, "Jesus of

Nazareth[d] is passing by." [38]Then he shouted, "Jesus, Son of David, have mercy on me!" [39]Those who were in front sternly ordered him to be quiet; but he shouted even more loudly, "Son of David, have mercy on me!" [40]Jesus stood still and ordered the man to be brought to him; and when he came near, he asked him, [41]"What do you want me to do for you?" He said, "Lord, let me see again." [42]Jesus said to him, "Receive your sight; your faith has saved you." [43]Immediately he regained his sight and followed him, glorifying God; and all the people, when they saw it, praised God.

A blind beggar hears a commotion. He learns that Jesus of Nazareth is passing by. He shouts out a plea for mercy. No one can quiet him. He is insistent. Jesus asks him to name the particular mercy he seeks. And he tells him that he wants to see. Jesus restores his sight.

As he approached Jericho, a blind man was sitting by the roadside begging…Then he shouted, "Jesus, Son of David, have mercy on me!" 18:35, 38

…he [Jesus] asked him, "What do you want me to do for you?" He said, "Lord, let me see again." Jesus said to him, "Receive your sight; your faith has saved you." 18:40-42

Meditation: The blind man begs Jesus for mercy. It is a general prayer for mercy. In his dialogue with Jesus, the blind man specifies the mercy he seeks. He wants his sight restored. Jesus heals him. We can easily miss what is so obvious in this story, if we reduce it to a remarkable physical phenomenon. Much more is at work in the blind beggar and in us. The mercy of God enables both him and us to see. God's mercy opens our eyes. We perceive new things, because God's mercy has touched us.

Question: If I truly saw everything through the eyes of mercy, how different would the world and other people appear?

d   Gk *the Nazorean*

Let us pray: You opened the eyes of the blind, O Lord. Your mercy enabled them to see the wonders of your grace at work in the world and in their own lives. Open our eyes to the mystery of your light that scatters the darkness of our world and that will bring us, one day, to see the light of your face.

Luke 19

Jesus and Zacchaeus: 19:1-10

[1]He entered Jericho and was passing through it. [2]A man was there named Zacchaeus; he was a chief tax collector and was rich. [3]He was trying to see who Jesus was, but on account of the crowd he could not, because he was short in stature. [4]So he ran ahead and climbed a sycamore tree to see him, because he was going to pass that way. [5]When Jesus came to the place, he looked up and said to him, "Zacchaeus, hurry and come down; for I must stay at your house today." [6]So he hurried down and was happy to welcome him. [7]All who saw it began to grumble and said, "He has gone to be the guest of one who is a sinner." [8]Zacchaeus stood there and said to the Lord, "Look, half of my possessions, Lord, I will give to the poor; and if I have defrauded anyone of anything, I will pay back four times as much." [9]Then Jesus said to him, "Today salvation has come to this house, because he too is a son of Abraham. [10]For the Son of Man came to seek out and to save the lost."

The very human and touching story of Zacchaeus gives us a snapshot of how the mercy of God works in this world. Notice how Zacchaeus is "trying to see Jesus." (19:3) Mercy comes to those who seek the Lord. Even more, mercy comes to those who resolve to live differently by living mercifully. For Zacchaeus, this meant giving to the poor and providing restitution to those he had wronged.

When Jesus came to the place, he looked up and said to him, "Zacchaeus, hurry and come down; for I must stay at your house today." Zacchaeus said to the Lord, "Look, half of my possessions, Lord, I will give to the poor." …Then Jesus said to him, "Today salvation has come to this house, because he too is a son of Abraham." 19:5, 8-9

"For the Son of Man came to seek out and to save the lost." 19:10

Meditation: The story of Zacchaeus is a powerful example of the mercy of God at work in the world. The mercy of God changes lives, as it changed Zacchaeus' life. There is a happy ending for Zacchaeus. However, the last line of the story ought to capture our attention. Jesus describes the full scope of his mission of mercy as seeking out and saving the lost. That is the ringing affirmation of hope for all of us.

Question: If I had a completely firm sense of the presence of God's mercy in my life, how would that lead me to make changes in my life?

> **Let us pray:** Every day, O Lord, keep us searching to see who Jesus is. And when he finds us, move us to change and reshape our hearts as instruments of generous mercy. Firmly fix our hope in Jesus, who seeks out and saves the lost.

The Parable of the Ten Pounds: 19:11-27

[11]As they were listening to this, he went on to tell a parable, because he was near Jerusalem, and because they supposed that the kingdom of God was to appear immediately. [12]So he said, "A nobleman went to a distant country to get royal power for himself and then return. [13]He summoned ten of his slaves, and gave them ten pounds,[a] and said to them, 'Do business with these until I come back.' [14]But the citizens of his country hated him and sent a delegation after him, saying, 'We do not want this man to rule over us.' [15]When he returned, having received royal power, he ordered these slaves, to whom he had given the money, to be summoned so that he might find out what they had gained by trading. [16]The first came forward and said, 'Lord, your pound has made ten more pounds.' [17]He said to him, 'Well done, good slave! Because you have been trustworthy in a very small thing, take charge of ten cities.' [18]Then the second came, saying, 'Lord, your pound has made five pounds.' [19]He said to him, 'And you, rule over five cities.' [20]Then the other came, saying, 'Lord, here is your pound. I wrapped it up in a piece of cloth, [21]for I was afraid of you, because you are a harsh man; you take what you did not deposit, and reap what you did not sow.' [22]He said to him, 'I will judge you by your own words,

---

a   The mina, rendered here by *pound*, was about three months' wages for a laborer

you wicked slave! You knew, did you, that I was a harsh man, taking what I did not deposit and reaping what I did not sow? [23]Why then did you not put my money into the bank? Then when I returned, I could have collected it with interest.' [24]He said to the bystanders, 'Take the pound from him and give it to the one who has ten pounds.' [25](And they said to him, 'Lord, he has ten pounds!') [26]'I tell you, to all those who have, more will be given; but from those who have nothing, even what they have will be taken away. [27]But as for these enemies of mine who did not want me to be king over them—bring them here and slaughter them in my presence.'"

Jesus' Triumphal Entrance Into Jerusalem: 19:28-40

[28]After he had said this, he went on ahead, going up to Jerusalem.

[29]When he had come near Bethphage and Bethany, at the place called the Mount of Olives, he sent two of the disciples, [30]saying, "Go into the village ahead of you, and as you enter it you will find tied there a colt that has never been ridden. Untie it and bring it here. [31]If anyone asks you, 'Why are you untying it?' just say this, 'The Lord needs it.'" [32]So those who were sent departed and found it as he had told them. [33]As they were untying the colt, its owners asked them, "Why are you untying the colt?" [34]They said, "The Lord needs it." [35]Then they brought it to Jesus; and after throwing their cloaks on the colt, they set Jesus on it. [36]As he rode along, people kept spreading their cloaks on the road. [37]As he was now approaching the path down from the Mount of Olives, the whole multitude of the disciples began to praise God joyfully with a loud voice for all the deeds of power that they had seen, [38]saying, "Blessed is the king who comes in the name of the Lord! Peace in heaven, and glory in the highest heaven!"

[39]Some of the Pharisees in the crowd said to him, "Teacher, order your disciples to stop." [40]He answered, "I tell you, if these were silent, the stones would shout out."

Jesus Weeps Over Jerusalem: 19:41-44

[41]As he came near and saw the city, he wept over it, [42]saying, "If you, even you, had only recognized on this day the things that make for peace! But now they are hidden from your eyes. [43]Indeed, the days will come upon you, when your enemies will set up ramparts around you and surround you, and hem you in on every side. [44]They will crush you to the ground, you and your children within you, and they will not leave within you one stone upon another; because you did not recognize the time of your visitation from God."[b]

As Jesus approaches the city of Jerusalem, Luke tells us that he wept over it. With his compassionate and merciful heart, Jesus lets his feelings for the future fate of Jerusalem well up and find expression in his tears. This is a unique moment in the gospel that captures an unexpected dimension of God's mercy for his people.

As he came near and saw the city, he wept over it, saying, "If you, even you, had only recognized on this day the things that make for peace!...you did not recognize the time of your visitation from God." 19:41-42, 44

Meditation: As we saw earlier, God's mercy must be received and accepted for it to take hold in his people. Here, Jesus speaks of those who neglected, did not recognize, and, therefore, did not receive God's mercy. That rejection does not end the story. In the human heart of Jesus, God grieves for the loss of his people. His mercy continues and reaches through and beyond their rejection.

Question: What do the tears of Jesus tell me about the mercy of God?

Let us pray: Your mercy never abandons us, O Lord, even when we abandon your mercy. Let the tears of Jesus water the dry and cold regions of our hearts, so that we may finally recognize that your undying mercy offers us new life.

b   Gk lacks *from God*

Jesus Cleanses the Temple: 19:45-48

[45]Then he entered the temple and began to drive out those who were selling things there; [46]and he said, "It is written, 'My house shall be a house of prayer'; but you have made it a den of robbers."

[47]Every day he was teaching in the temple. The chief priests, the scribes, and the leaders of the people kept looking for a way to kill him; [48]but they did not find anything they could do, for all the people were spellbound by what they heard.

Luke 20

Religious Leaders Question the Authority of Jesus: 20:1-8

[1]One day, as he was teaching the people in the temple and telling the good news, the chief priests and the scribes came with the elders [2]and said to him, "Tell us, by what authority are you doing these things? Who is it who gave you this authority?" [3]He answered them, "I will also ask you a question, and you tell me: [4]Did the baptism of John come from heaven, or was it of human origin?" [5]They discussed it with one another, saying, "If we say, 'From heaven,' he will say, 'Why did you not believe him?' [6]But if we say, 'Of human origin,' all the people will stone us; for they are convinced that John was a prophet." [7]So they answered that they did not know where it came from. [8]Then Jesus said to them, "Neither will I tell you by what authority I am doing these things."

The Parable of the Wicked Tenants: 20:9-19

[9]He began to tell the people this parable: "A man planted a vineyard, and leased it to tenants, and went to another country for a long time. [10]When the season came, he sent a slave to the tenants in order that they might give him his share of the produce of the vineyard; but the tenants beat him and sent him away empty-handed. [11]Next he sent another slave; that one also they beat and insulted and sent away empty-handed. [12]And he sent still a third; this one also they wounded and threw out. [13]Then the owner of the vineyard said, 'What shall I do? I will send my beloved son; perhaps they will respect him.' [14]But when the tenants saw him, they discussed it among themselves and said, 'This is the heir; let us kill him so that the inheritance may be ours.' [15]So they threw him out of the vineyard and killed him. What then will the owner of the vineyard do to them? [16]He will come and destroy those tenants and give the vineyard to others." When they heard this, they said, "Heaven forbid!" [17]But he looked at them and said, "What then does this text mean: 'The stone that the builders rejected has become the cornerstone'?[a]

a   Or *keystone*

¹⁸Everyone who falls on that stone will be broken to pieces; and it will crush anyone on whom it falls." ¹⁹When the scribes and chief priests realized that he had told this parable against them, they wanted to lay hands on him at that very hour, but they feared the people.

When the owner of the vineyard sends representative after representative—and finally his son—to collect his portion of the vintage, the tenants treat them cruelly and eventually murder the son. The parable refers to God sending the prophets to his people, prophets who were rejected. Finally, God sends his only son who is not only rejected but killed. The parable can be read as story of God's many merciful interventions that are rebuffed and, then, finally rejected in the rejection of his son.

"And he sent yet a third; this one also they wounded and threw out. Then the owner of the vineyard said, 'I will send my beloved son…' But when the tenants saw him, they…said, 'This is the heir; let us kill him so that the inheritance may be ours.' So they threw him out of the vineyard and killed him." 20:12-14

Meditation: The contrast could not be starker between the merciful interventions of God in sending the prophets and, finally, his own beloved son, and the cruel and merciless response to that goodness. The story is certainly about rejection. Even more, it is about a lack of mercy in hearts incapable of receiving what God offers. The tenants—and we with them—are frighteningly capable of falling away from God's merciful outreach, especially when we are caught by our own narrow and self-centered concerns, *so that the inheritance may be ours.*

Question: How do especially difficult and troublesome temptations push us to rely more and more completely upon the mercy of God?

Let us pray: Never let us fail, O Lord, to receive your mercy into our lives. Remove whatever within us that could block us from gratefully and

> graciously receiving what you offer us. Keep us
> mindful of our weakness, so that we may depend
> ever more on you alone.

The Question About Paying Taxes: 20:20-26

[20]So they watched him and sent spies who pretended to be
honest, in order to trap him by what he said, so as to hand
him over to the jurisdiction and authority of the governor.
[21]So they asked him, "Teacher, we know that you are right
in what you say and teach, and you show deference to no
one, but teach the way of God in accordance with truth. [22]Is
it lawful for us to pay taxes to the emperor, or not?" [23]But he
perceived their craftiness and said to them, [24]"Show me a denarius. Whose head and whose title does it bear?" They said,
"The emperor's." [25]He said to them, "Then give to the emperor
the things that are the emperor's, and to God the things that
are God's." [26]And they were not able in the presence of the
people to trap him by what he said; and being amazed by his
answer, they became silent.

The Question About the Resurrection: 20:27-40

[27]Some Sadducees, those who say there is no resurrection,
came to him [28]and asked him a question, "Teacher, Moses
wrote for us that if a man's brother dies, leaving a wife but
no children, the man[b] shall marry the widow and raise up
children for his brother. [29]Now there were seven brothers;
the first married, and died childless; [30]then the second [31]and
the third married her, and so in the same way all seven died
childless. [32]Finally the woman also died. [33]In the resurrection,
therefore, whose wife will the woman be? For the seven had
married her."

[34]Jesus said to them, "Those who belong to this age marry
and are given in marriage; [35]but those who are considered
worthy of a place in that age and in the resurrection from
the dead neither marry nor are given in marriage. [36]Indeed
they cannot die anymore, because they are like angels and are
children of God, being children of the resurrection. [37]And

b   Gk *his brother*

the fact that the dead are raised Moses himself showed, in the story about the bush, where he speaks of the Lord as the God of Abraham, the God of Isaac, and the God of Jacob. ³⁸Now he is God not of the dead, but of the living; for to him all of them are alive." ³⁹Then some of the scribes answered, "Teacher, you have spoken well." ⁴⁰For they no longer dared to ask him another question.

The Question About David's Son: 20:41-44

⁴¹Then he said to them, "How can they say that the Messiahᶜ is David's son? ⁴²For David himself says in the book of Psalms, 'The Lord said to my Lord, "Sit at my right hand, ⁴³until I make your enemies your footstool."' ⁴⁴David thus calls him Lord; so how can he be his son?"

Jesus Denounces the Scribes: 20:45-47

⁴⁵In the hearing of all the people he said to theᵈ disciples, ⁴⁶"Beware of the scribes, who like to walk around in long robes, and love to be greeted with respect in the marketplaces, and to have the best seats in the synagogues and places of honor at banquets. ⁴⁷They devour widows' houses and for the sake of appearance say long prayers. They will receive the greater condemnation."

c   Or *the Christ*
d   Other ancient authorities read *his*

Luke 21

The Widow's Offering: 21:1-4

[1]He looked up and saw rich people putting their gifts into the treasury; [2]he also saw a poor widow put in two small copper coins. [3]He said, "Truly I tell you, this poor widow has put in more than all of them; [4]for all of them have contributed out of their abundance, but she out of her poverty has put in all she had to live on."

The contrast between rich people giving money from their surplus and a poor widow giving an offering from her basic sustenance does not directly speak to the theme of mercy. It does, however, address an important dimension of mercy—generosity. Our mercy is not real mercy, unless it is generous.

"…a poor widow put in two small copper coins…for all of them have contributed out of their abundance, but she out of her poverty has put in all she had to live on." 21:2, 4

Meditation: Generosity in making contributions to good causes or offering mercy to others is a sign of freedom. There is no fear of being deprived of resources, and there is no fear of too much mercy, of being "too soft" on others. This free and full generosity represents not simply something that is given but one's very self offered to others.

Question: What would make me more generous as I try to bring God's merciful presence to the world?

Let us pray: In our measured out world, inspire us, O Lord, with your generosity to embrace a like willingness to share your mercy freely and abundantly. Save us from the fear of giving away too much by our sure knowledge that you always outdo us in your generosity.

The Destruction of the Temple Foretold: 21:5-6

[5]When some were speaking about the temple, how it was adorned with beautiful stones and gifts dedicated to God, he said, [6]"As for these things that you see, the days will come when not one stone will be left upon another; all will be thrown down."

Jesus Speaks of the Future of the Temple and Jerusalem, of Coming Persecutions, and of the Coming of the Son of Man, and the Need to be Vigilant: 21:7-38

[7]They asked him, "Teacher, when will this be, and what will be the sign that this is about to take place?" [8]And he said, "Beware that you are not led astray; for many will come in my name and say, 'I am he!'[a] and, 'The time is near!'[b] Do not go after them.

[9]"When you hear of wars and insurrections, do not be terrified; for these things must take place first, but the end will not follow immediately." [10]Then he said to them, "Nation will rise against nation, and kingdom against kingdom; [11]there will be great earthquakes, and in various places famines and plagues; and there will be dreadful portents and great signs from heaven.

[12]"But before all this occurs, they will arrest you and persecute you; they will hand you over to synagogues and prisons, and you will be brought before kings and governors because of my name. [13]This will give you an opportunity to testify. [14]So make up your minds not to prepare your defense in advance; [15]for I will give you words[c] and a wisdom that none of your opponents will be able to withstand or contradict. [16]You will be betrayed even by parents and brothers, by relatives and friends; and they will put some of you to death. [17]You will be hated by all because of my name. [18]But not a hair of your head will perish. [19]By your endurance you will gain your souls.

a   Gk *I am*
b   Or *at hand*
c   Gk *a mouth*

[20]"When you see Jerusalem surrounded by armies, then know that its desolation has come near.[d] [21]Then those in Judea must flee to the mountains, and those inside the city must leave it, and those out in the country must not enter it; [22]for these are days of vengeance, as a fulfillment of all that is written. [23]Woe to those who are pregnant and to those who are nursing infants in those days! For there will be great distress on the earth and wrath against this people; [24]they will fall by the edge of the sword and be taken away as captives among all nations; and Jerusalem will be trampled on by the Gentiles, until the times of the Gentiles are fulfilled.

[25]"There will be signs in the sun, the moon, and the stars, and on the earth distress among nations confused by the roaring of the sea and the waves. [26]People will faint from fear and foreboding of what is coming upon the world, for the powers of the heavens will be shaken. [27]Then they will see 'the Son of Man coming in a cloud' with power and great glory. [28]Now when these things begin to take place, stand up and raise your heads, because your redemption is drawing near."

[29]Then he told them a parable: "Look at the fig tree and all the trees; [30]as soon as they sprout leaves you can see for yourselves and know that summer is already near. [31]So also, when you see these things taking place, you know that the kingdom of God is near. [32]Truly I tell you, this generation will not pass away until all things have taken place. [33]Heaven and earth will pass away, but my words will not pass away.

[34]"Be on guard so that your hearts are not weighed down with dissipation and drunkenness and the worries of this life, and that day does not catch you unexpectedly, [35]like a trap. For it will come upon all who live on the face of the whole earth. [36]Be alert at all times, praying that you may have the strength to escape all these things that will take place, and to stand before the Son of Man."

[37]Every day he was teaching in the temple, and at night he would go out and spend the night on the Mount of Olives, as

it was called. [38]And all the people would get up early in the morning to listen to him in the temple.

Luke 22

The Plot to Kill Jesus: 22:1-6

[1]Now the festival of Unleavened Bread, which is called the Passover, was near. [2]The chief priests and the scribes were looking for a way to put Jesus[a] to death, for they were afraid of the people.

[3]Then Satan entered into Judas called Iscariot, who was one of the twelve; [4]he went away and conferred with the chief priests and officers of the temple police about how he might betray him to them. [5]They were greatly pleased and agreed to give him money. [6]So he consented and began to look for an opportunity to betray him to them when no crowd was present.

The Preparations for the Passover: 22:7-13

[7]Then came the day of Unleavened Bread, on which the Passover lamb had to be sacrificed. [8]So Jesus[b] sent Peter and John, saying, "Go and prepare the Passover meal for us that we may eat it." [9]They asked him, "Where do you want us to make preparations for it?" [10]"Listen," he said to them, "when you have entered the city, a man carrying a jar of water will meet you; follow him into the house he enters [11]and say to the owner of the house, 'The teacher asks you, "Where is the guest room, where I may eat the Passover with my disciples?"' [12]He will show you a large room upstairs, already furnished. Make preparations for us there." [13]So they went and found everything as he had told them; and they prepared the Passover meal.

The Institution of the Lord's Supper: 22:14-23

[14]When the hour came, he took his place at the table, and the apostles with him. [15]He said to them, "I have eagerly desired to eat this Passover with you before I suffer; [16]for I tell you, I will not eat it[c] until it is fulfilled in the kingdom of God." [17]Then he took a cup, and after giving thanks he said, "Take

a   Gk *him*
b   Gk *he*
c   Other ancient authorities read *never eat it again*

this and divide it among yourselves; [18]for I tell you that from now on I will not drink of the fruit of the vine until the kingdom of God comes." [19]Then he took a loaf of bread, and when he had given thanks, he broke it and gave it to them, saying, "This is my body, which is given for you. Do this in remembrance of me." [20]And he did the same with the cup after supper, saying, "This cup that is poured out for you is the new covenant in my blood.[d] [21]But see, the one who betrays me is with me, and his hand is on the table. [22]For the Son of Man is going as it has been determined, but woe to that one by whom he is betrayed!" [23]Then they began to ask one another which one of them it could be who would do this.

When Jesus gathers his disciples to celebrate the Passover the night before he dies, he gives them a lasting memorial of his merciful love by offering them bread and wine that become his body and blood and that will be offered up for them. As often as they do this in remembrance of him, they—and we today—recall Jesus' mercy.

Then he took a loaf of bread, and when he had given thanks, he broke it and gave it to them, saying, "This is my body, which is given for you. Do this in remembrance of me." And he did the same with the cup after supper, saying, "This cup that is poured out for you is the new covenant in my blood." 22:19-20

Meditation: The mercy of God is clearly manifested on the cross of Jesus. His self-sacrificing love brings us the forgiveness of our sins and our complete healing and transformation. The Eucharist is the effective sign of God's mercy. It effects what it signifies.

Question: What would help me to both receive and live the Eucharist as the sacrament of God's mercy? What would this look like in my daily life?

Let us pray: When we share in your Eucharist, O Lord, keep us mindful of the love and mercy that comes to us in these sacred elements. May our

d   Other ancient authorities lack, in whole or in part, verses 19b–20 (*which is given . . . in my blood*)

sacramental meeting with Jesus Christ crucified, our merciful savior, enable us to carry his mercy to a world in need.

A Dispute About Greatness: 22:24-30

[24]A dispute also arose among them as to which one of them was to be regarded as the greatest. [25]But he said to them, "The kings of the Gentiles lord it over them; and those in authority over them are called benefactors. [26]But not so with you; rather the greatest among you must become like the youngest, and the leader like one who serves. [27]For who is greater, the one who is at the table or the one who serves? Is it not the one at the table? But I am among you as one who serves.

[28]"You are those who have stood by me in my trials; [29]and I confer on you, just as my Father has conferred on me, a kingdom, [30]so that you may eat and drink at my table in my kingdom, and you will sit on thrones judging the twelve tribes of Israel.

Jesus Predicts Peter's Denial: 22:31-34

[31]"Simon, Simon, listen! Satan has demanded[e] to sift all of you like wheat, [32]but I have prayed for you that your own faith may not fail; and you, when once you have turned back, strengthen your brothers." [33]And he said to him, "Lord, I am ready to go with you to prison and to death!" [34]Jesus[f] said, "I tell you, Peter, the cock will not crow this day, until you have denied three times that you know me."

Provisions for the Mission: 22:35-38

[35]He said to them, "When I sent you out without a purse, bag, or sandals, did you lack anything?" They said, "No, not a thing." [36]He said to them, "But now, the one who has a purse must take it, and likewise a bag. And the one who has no sword must sell his cloak and buy one. [37]For I tell you, this scripture must be fulfilled in me, 'And he was counted among the lawless'; and indeed what is written about me is being

e   Or *has obtained permission*
f   Gk *He*

fulfilled." ³⁸They said, "Lord, look, here are two swords." He replied, "It is enough."

Jesus Prays in the Garden on the Mount of Olives: 22:39-46

³⁹He came out and went, as was his custom, to the Mount of Olives; and the disciples followed him. ⁴⁰When he reached the place, he said to them, "Pray that you may not come into the time of trial."ᵍ ⁴¹Then he withdrew from them about a stone's throw, knelt down, and prayed, ⁴²"Father, if you are willing, remove this cup from me; yet, not my will but yours be done." [[⁴³Then an angel from heaven appeared to him and gave him strength. ⁴⁴In his anguish he prayed more earnestly, and his sweat became like great drops of blood falling down on the ground.]]ʰ ⁴⁵When he got up from prayer, he came to the disciples and found them sleeping because of grief, ⁴⁶and he said to them, "Why are you sleeping? Get up and pray that you may not come into the time of trial."ⁱ

The prayer of Jesus in the garden on the night before he dies reveals a moment of unparallel intimacy with his heavenly Father. Jesus is in anguish, and he struggles. He prays to be mercifully delivered. Even more, he prays that his Father's will be accomplished in him. This particular prayer of Jesus opens new horizons for our prayers for mercy.

"Father, if you are willing, remove this cup from me; yet, not my will but yours be done." 22:42

Meditation: When Jesus prays to his Father, he does so with complete confidence and trust that he will be heard. Our own prayer should be the same. Jesus' prayer wholeheartedly relies on his heavenly Father and identifies a specific request for mercy—*remove this cup from me*. Still, he recognizes that however his specific request is or is not fulfilled, his Father's will is certainly directed toward mercy for him and for all who ask for it. When we enter Jesus'

g   Or *into temptation*
h   Other ancient authorities lack verses 43 and 44
i   Or *into temptation*

prayer in the garden, we begin to understand for ourselves the relationship between trust and mercy.

Question: What do I do or what can I do when the mercy of God seems so remote from me?

> **Let us pray:** Increase our trust in you, O Lord, so that we may hold confidently to your holy will, which always brings your mercy into our lives, even in ways we cannot expect or imagine.

The Betrayal and Arrest of Jesus: 22:47-53

[47]While he was still speaking, suddenly a crowd came, and the one called Judas, one of the twelve, was leading them. He approached Jesus to kiss him; [48]but Jesus said to him, "Judas, is it with a kiss that you are betraying the Son of Man?" [49]When those who were around him saw what was coming, they asked, "Lord, should we strike with the sword?" [50]Then one of them struck the slave of the high priest and cut off his right ear. [51]But Jesus said, "No more of this!" And he touched his ear and healed him. [52]Then Jesus said to the chief priests, the officers of the temple police, and the elders who had come for him, "Have you come out with swords and clubs as if I were a bandit? [53]When I was with you day after day in the temple, you did not lay hands on me. But this is your hour, and the power of darkness!"

Peter Denies Jesus: 22:54-62

[54]Then they seized him and led him away, bringing him into the high priest's house. But Peter was following at a distance. [55]When they had kindled a fire in the middle of the court-yard and sat down together, Peter sat among them. [56]Then a servant-girl, seeing him in the firelight, stared at him and said, "This man also was with him." [57]But he denied it, saying, "Woman, I do not know him." [58]A little later someone else, on seeing him, said, "You also are one of them." But Peter said, "Man, I am not!" [59]Then about an hour later still another kept insisting, "Surely this man also was with him; for he is a Galilean." [60]But Peter said, "Man, I do not know what you are

talking about!" At that moment, while he was still speaking, the cock crowed. [61]The Lord turned and looked at Peter. Then Peter remembered the word of the Lord, how he had said to him, "Before the cock crows today, you will deny me three times." [62]And he went out and wept bitterly.

The Mocking and Beating of Jesus: 22:63-65

[63]Now the men who were holding Jesus began to mock him and beat him; [64]they also blindfolded him and kept asking him, "Prophesy! Who is it that struck you?" [65]They kept heaping many other insults on him.

Jesus Before the Council: 22:66-71

[66]When day came, the assembly of the elders of the people, both chief priests and scribes, gathered together, and they brought him to their council. [67]They said, "If you are the Messiah,[j] tell us." He replied, "If I tell you, you will not believe; [68]and if I question you, you will not answer. [69]But from now on the Son of Man will be seated at the right hand of the power of God." [70]All of them asked, "Are you, then, the Son of God?" He said to them, "You say that I am." [71]Then they said, "What further testimony do we need? We have heard it ourselves from his own lips!"

j   Or *the Christ*

Luke 23

Jesus Before Pilate: 23:1-5

[1]Then the assembly rose as a body and brought Jesus[a] before Pilate. [2]They began to accuse him, saying, "We found this man perverting our nation, forbidding us to pay taxes to the emperor, and saying that he himself is the Messiah, a king."[b] [3]Then Pilate asked him, "Are you the king of the Jews?" He answered, "You say so." [4]Then Pilate said to the chief priests and the crowds, "I find no basis for an accusation against this man." [5]But they were insistent and said, "He stirs up the people by teaching throughout all Judea, from Galilee where he began even to this place."

Jesus Before Herod: 23:6-12

[6]When Pilate heard this, he asked whether the man was a Galilean. [7]And when he learned that he was under Herod's jurisdiction, he sent him off to Herod, who was himself in Jerusalem at that time. [8]When Herod saw Jesus, he was very glad, for he had been wanting to see him for a long time, because he had heard about him and was hoping to see him perform some sign. [9]He questioned him at some length, but Jesus[c] gave him no answer. [10]The chief priests and the scribes stood by, vehemently accusing him. [11]Even Herod with his soldiers treated him with contempt and mocked him; then he put an elegant robe on him, and sent him back to Pilate. [12]That same day Herod and Pilate became friends with each other; before this they had been enemies.

Jesus Sentenced to Death: 23:13-25

[13]Pilate then called together the chief priests, the leaders, and the people, [14]and said to them, "You brought me this man as one who was perverting the people; and here I have examined him in your presence and have not found this man guilty of any of your charges against him. [15]Neither has Herod, for he sent him back to us. Indeed, he has done noth-

a   Gk *him*
b   Or *is an anointed king*
c   Gk *he*

ing to deserve death. ¹⁶I will therefore have him flogged and release him."ᵈ

¹⁸Then they all shouted out together, "Away with this fellow! Release Barabbas for us!" ¹⁹(This was a man who had been put in prison for an insurrection that had taken place in the city, and for murder.) ²⁰Pilate, wanting to release Jesus, addressed them again; ²¹but they kept shouting, "Crucify, crucify him!" ²²A third time he said to them, "Why, what evil has he done? I have found in him no ground for the sentence of death; I will therefore have him flogged and then release him." ²³But they kept urgently demanding with loud shouts that he should be crucified; and their voices prevailed. ²⁴So Pilate gave his verdict that their demand should be granted. ²⁵He released the man they asked for, the one who had been put in prison for insurrection and murder, and he handed Jesus over as they wished.

Pilate does not find Jesus guilty of a capital crime. He wants to release him whether as a matter of justice and fairness or according to the custom of granting mercy at the time of the feast. Three times, those who want Jesus crucified shout Pilate down. He is worn down. Eventually, Pilate grants mercy to Barabbas and condemns Jesus to death.

Pilate…said to them, "You brought this man as one who was perverting the people; and here I have examined him in your presence and have not found this man guilty of any of your charges against him." 23:13-14

But they kept urgently demanding with loud shouts that he should be crucified; and their voices prevailed. So Pilate gave his verdict that their demand should be granted. 23:23-24

Meditation: The death of Jesus for us is for the forgiveness of our sins and for our liberation from death. It is God's great act of mercy extended to us from the wood of the Cross. Paradoxically, the proximate cause of Jesus' death is the lack of mercy among the religious leaders of the time

d   Here, or after verse 19, other ancient authorities add verse 17, *Now he was obliged to release someone for them at the festival*

as well as a lack of mercy on Pilate's part. God, however, is undaunted. He transforms their lack of human mercy into the divine and merciful source of our life and our salvation on the Cross.

Question: How can we move confidently through a world that seems devoid of mercy? What do we do to challenge mercilessness?

> **Let us pray:** When dark and merciless forces seem to overwhelm us, O Lord, reassure us of your merciful presence within us. Enable us to understand that you have the power to transform darkness into light, death into life, and unjust condemnation into the glorious manifestation of your mercy.

The Crucifixion of Jesus: 23:26-43

[26]As they led him away, they seized a man, Simon of Cyrene, who was coming from the country, and they laid the cross on him, and made him carry it behind Jesus. [27]A great number of the people followed him, and among them were women who were beating their breasts and wailing for him. [28]But Jesus turned to them and said, "Daughters of Jerusalem, do not weep for me, but weep for yourselves and for your children. [29]For the days are surely coming when they will say, 'Blessed are the barren, and the wombs that never bore, and the breasts that never nursed.' [30]Then they will begin to say to the mountains, 'Fall on us'; and to the hills, 'Cover us.' [31]For if they do this when the wood is green, what will happen when it is dry?"

[32]Two others also, who were criminals, were led away to be put to death with him. [33]When they came to the place that is called The Skull, they crucified Jesus[e] there with the criminals, one on his right and one on his left. [[[34]Then Jesus said, "Father, forgive them; for they do not know what they

e   Gk *him*

are doing."]]ᶠ And they cast lots to divide his clothing. ³⁵And the people stood by, watching; but the leaders scoffed at him, saying, "He saved others; let him save himself if he is the Messiahᵍ of God, his chosen one!" ³⁶The soldiers also mocked him, coming up and offering him sour wine, ³⁷and saying, "If you are the King of the Jews, save yourself!" ³⁸There was also an inscription over him,ʰ "This is the King of the Jews."

³⁹One of the criminals who were hanged there kept deridingⁱ him and saying, "Are you not the Messiah?ʲ Save yourself and us!" ⁴⁰But the other rebuked him, saying, "Do you not fear God, since you are under the same sentence of condemnation? ⁴¹And we indeed have been condemned justly, for we are getting what we deserve for our deeds, but this man has done nothing wrong." ⁴²Then he said, "Jesus, remember me when you come intoᵏ your kingdom." ⁴³He replied, "Truly I tell you, today you will be with me in Paradise."

The death of Jesus is the great sign of God's mercy that breaks into our world of sin and death. In different ways, the crucifixion of Jesus also reveals aspects of the mercy of God.

A great number of the people followed him, and among them were women who were beating their breasts and wailing for him. But Jesus turned to them and said, "Daughters of Jerusalem, do not weep for me but weep for yourselves and for your children." 23:27-28

Meditation: Pain and suffering can be very self-absorbing. Jesus, carrying his painful cross, breaks out and beyond his suffering in a word of compassion and mercy for the grieving women. In and through his suffering, he connects with the suffering of others, with our suffering.

f   Other ancient authorities lack the sentence *Then Jesus . . . what they are doing*
g   Or *the Christ*
h   Other ancient authorities add *written in Greek and Latin and Hebrew* (that is, *Aramaic*)
i   Or *blaspheming*
j   Or *the Christ*
k   Other ancient authorities read *in*

…they crucified Jesus there with the criminals, one on his right and one on his left. Then Jesus said, "Father, forgive them; for they do not know what they are doing." 23:33-34

> **Meditation**: Unbidden, Jesus offers his mercy and forgiveness to those who crucify him. Saint Aelred of Rievaulx marvels at the merciful forgiveness of Jesus who not only forgives those who crucify him but also offers an excuse for their actions—*for they do not know what they are doing.*

Then he [one of the criminals] said, "Jesus, remember me when you come into your kingdom. He replied, "Truly I tell you, today you will be with me in Paradise." 23:42-43

> **Meditation**: Again, in middle of his own suffering, Jesus reaches out to the repentant criminal who wants a share in the Kingdom of God. In his mercy, Jesus grants his request. We also begin to understand there are no limits set on God's mercy. It is never too late to let God's mercy take hold of our lives. Just as everything seems to fold and collapse both for Jesus and the criminal crucified with him, a singular promise emerges.
>
> *Today you will be with me in Paradise.* Mercy triumphs on the cross of Jesus.
>
> **Question:** In light of God's mercy, how does the suffering and death of Jesus on the cross illuminate and redirect my personal suffering?

> **Let us pray:** O Lord, let us walk the road with Jesus, the road that leads to the cross. In this way, we will discover the depth and breadth of your mercy given to us. We will know that your mercy is without limit. Create within us a heart to be merciful as you are merciful in our own limita-

tions and suffering and always ready to extend
mercy to all who ask us.

The Death and Burial of Jesus: 23:44-56

[44]It was now about noon, and darkness came over the whole
land[l] until three in the afternoon, [45]while the sun's light
failed;[m] and the curtain of the temple was torn in two. [46]Then
Jesus, crying with a loud voice, said, "Father, into your hands
I commend my spirit." Having said this, he breathed his last.
[47]When the centurion saw what had taken place, he praised
God and said, "Certainly this man was innocent."[n] [48]And
when all the crowds who had gathered there for this specta-
cle saw what had taken place, they returned home, beating
their breasts. [49]But all his acquaintances, including the wom-
en who had followed him from Galilee, stood at a distance,
watching these things.

[50]Now there was a good and righteous man named Joseph,
who, though a member of the council, [51]had not agreed to
their plan and action. He came from the Jewish town of
Arimathea, and he was waiting expectantly for the kingdom
of God. [52]This man went to Pilate and asked for the body of
Jesus. [53]Then he took it down, wrapped it in a linen cloth, and
laid it in a rock-hewn tomb where no one had ever been laid.
[54]It was the day of Preparation, and the sabbath was beginning.[o] [55]The women who had come with him from Galilee
followed, and they saw the tomb and how his body was laid.
[56]Then they returned, and prepared spices and ointments.

On the sabbath they rested according to the commandment.

When Jesus dies, he does so in a great act of surrender. He entrusts
himself entirely into the merciful hands of his Father. The final act
of his earthly life is to abandon himself into the hidden mystery of
God. His self-sacrifice is his gift of himself to his Father and to us. This
complete act of total trust so affects a Roman and pagan centurion
that he confesses Jesus' innocence and praises God.

l   Or earth
m   Or the sun was eclipsed. Other ancient authorities read the sun was darkened
n   Or righteous
o   Gk was dawning

Then Jesus, crying with a loud voice, said, "Father, into your hands I commend my spirit"…When the centurion saw what had taken place, he praised God and said, "Certainly this man was innocent." 23:46-48

Meditation: Once again, the close relationship between trust and mercy becomes evident on the cross of Jesus. Trust turns to God's mercy and is never disappointed, even though the exact outcome of our plea may not be immediately clear. Trust relies on the promise of God's merciful presence and on that alone.

Question: How can I practice surrender, so that at the end of my life, with Jesus, I can surrender myself entirely to God's mercy?

Let us pray: May we never cease to trust you, O Lord. May we never cease to entrust ourselves to you. Allow your promise of mercy to lead us forward, even when we cannot clearly see our destination. Then, when we have completed our journey, we will clearly see you and be embraced by your love.

Luke 24

The Resurrection of Jesus: 24:1-12

¹But on the first day of the week, at early dawn, they came to the tomb, taking the spices that they had prepared. ²They found the stone rolled away from the tomb, ³but when they went in, they did not find the body.ᵃ ⁴While they were perplexed about this, suddenly two men in dazzling clothes stood beside them. ⁵The womenᵇ were terrified and bowed their faces to the ground, but the menᶜ said to them, "Why do you look for the living among the dead? He is not here, but has risen.ᵈ ⁶Remember how he told you, while he was still in Galilee, ⁷that the Son of Man must be handed over to sinners, and be crucified, and on the third day rise again." ⁸Then they remembered his words, ⁹and returning from the tomb, they told all this to the eleven and to all the rest. ¹⁰Now it was Mary Magdalene, Joanna, Mary the mother of James, and the other women with them who told this to the apostles. ¹¹But these words seemed to them an idle tale, and they did not believe them. ¹²But Peter got up and ran to the tomb; stooping and looking in, he saw the linen cloths by themselves; then he went home, amazed at what had happened.ᵉ

Meeting the Two Disciples on the Way to Emmaus: 24:13-35

¹³Now on that same day two of them were going to a village called Emmaus, about seven milesᶠ from Jerusalem, ¹⁴and talking with each other about all these things that had happened. ¹⁵While they were talking and discussing, Jesus himself came near and went with them, ¹⁶but their eyes were kept from recognizing him. ¹⁷And he said to them, "What are you discussing with each other while you walk along?" They stood still, looking sad.ᵍ ¹⁸Then one of them, whose name was Cleopas, answered him, "Are you the only stranger in Jerusalem who does not know the things that have taken

a   Other ancient authorities add *of the Lord Jesus*
b   Gk *They*
c   Gk *but they*
d   Other ancient authorities lack *He is not here, but has risen*
e   Other ancient authorities lack verse 12
f   Gk *sixty stadia;* other ancient authorities read *a hundred sixty stadia*
g   Other ancient authorities read *walk along, looking sad?"*

place there in these days?" ¹⁹He asked them, "What things?"
They replied, "The things about Jesus of Nazareth,ʰ who was
a prophet mighty in deed and word before God and all the
people, ²⁰and how our chief priests and leaders handed him
over to be condemned to death and crucified him. ²¹But we
had hoped that he was the one to redeem Israel.ⁱ Yes, and
besides all this, it is now the third day since these things took
place. ²²Moreover, some women of our group astounded us.
They were at the tomb early this morning, ²³and when they
did not find his body there, they came back and told us that
they had indeed seen a vision of angels who said that he was
alive. ²⁴Some of those who were with us went to the tomb and
found it just as the women had said; but they did not see him."
²⁵Then he said to them, "Oh, how foolish you are, and how
slow of heart to believe all that the prophets have declared!
²⁶Was it not necessary that the Messiahʲ should suffer these
things and then enter into his glory?" ²⁷Then beginning with
Moses and all the prophets, he interpreted to them the things
about himself in all the scriptures.

²⁸As they came near the village to which they were going, he
walked ahead as if he were going on. ²⁹But they urged him
strongly, saying, "Stay with us, because it is almost evening
and the day is now nearly over." So he went in to stay with
them. ³⁰When he was at the table with them, he took bread,
blessed and broke it, and gave it to them. ³¹Then their eyes
were opened, and they recognized him; and he vanished
from their sight. ³²They said to each other, "Were not our
hearts burning within usᵏ while he was talking to us on the
road, while he was opening the scriptures to us?" ³³That same
hour they got up and returned to Jerusalem; and they found
the eleven and their companions gathered together. ³⁴They
were saying, "The Lord has risen indeed, and he has appeared
to Simon!" ³⁵Then they told what had happened on the road,
and how he had been made known to them in the breaking
of the bread.

h   Other ancient authorities read *Jesus the Nazorean*
i   Or *to set Israel free*
j   Or *the Christ*
k   Other ancient authorities lack *within us*

In this famous passage that is unique to Luke, there is no explicit mention of mercy. It seems to be the story of two disheartened disciples whose spirits are lifted up by their encounter with the risen Jesus. Mercy, however, is embedded in the text in a surprising way, which echoes the beginning of Luke's gospel.

Then he said to them, "Oh, how foolish you are, and how slow of heart to believe all that the prophets have declared! Was it not necessary that the Messiah should suffer these things and then enter into his glory?" Then beginning with Moses and all the prophets, he interpreted to them the things about himself in all the scriptures. 24:25-27

Meditation: At the center of the encounter of Jesus and the two disciples on their way to Emmaus is the explanation that Jesus gives of his suffering and death in light of the whole history of Israel and the prophets. With this wide expanse of history, Jesus demonstrates to the two disciples what Mary had proclaimed in the very first chapter of the gospel: *His mercy is for those who fear him from generation to generation* (1:50). God's mercy has been at work in the world from generation to generation, and culminates in the death and resurrection of Jesus. His explanation to the disciples leaves their hearts on fire: *"Were not our hearts burning within us while he was talking to us on the road, while he was opening the scriptures to us?"* (24:32) Now, they are prepared to make this same proclamation of mercy and salvation as they return to Jerusalem: *Then they told what had happened on the road, and how he had been made known to them in the breaking of the bread.* (24:35)

Question: Do I sufficiently reflect upon how God's mercy has taken hold of my life and our world? Or, do I just assume that God is merciful?

Let us pray: Walk with us, O Lord, and open our minds to understand the story of your mercy at work in the world and in our lives. Through your suffering and death, you lead us through sin and

> death to forgiveness and new life. Your mercies are countless, your love without end. May glory, praise, and thanksgiving be yours now and forever.

Jesus Appears to His Disciples, Sends Them on Mission, and Ascends to Heaven: 24:36-53

[36]While they were talking about this, Jesus himself stood among them and said to them, "Peace be with you."[l] [37]They were startled and terrified, and thought that they were seeing a ghost. [38]He said to them, "Why are you frightened, and why do doubts arise in your hearts? [39]Look at my hands and my feet; see that it is I myself. Touch me and see; for a ghost does not have flesh and bones as you see that I have." [40]And when he had said this, he showed them his hands and his feet.[m] [41]While in their joy they were disbelieving and still wondering, he said to them, "Have you anything here to eat?" [42]They gave him a piece of broiled fish, [43]and he took it and ate in their presence.

[44]Then he said to them, "These are my words that I spoke to you while I was still with you—that everything written about me in the law of Moses, the prophets, and the psalms must be fulfilled." [45]Then he opened their minds to understand the scriptures, [46]and he said to them, "Thus it is written, that the Messiah[n] is to suffer and to rise from the dead on the third day, [47]and that repentance and forgiveness of sins is to be proclaimed in his name to all nations, beginning from Jerusalem. [48]You are witnesses[o] of these things. [49]And see, I am sending upon you what my Father promised; so stay here in the city until you have been clothed with power from on high."

[50]Then he led them out as far as Bethany, and, lifting up his hands, he blessed them. [51]While he was blessing them, he withdrew from them and was carried up into heaven.[p] [52]And

l   Other ancient authorities lack *and said to them, "Peace be with you."*
m   Other ancient authorities lack verse 40
n   Or *the Christ*
o   Or *nations. Beginning from Jerusalem* [48] *you are witnesses*
p   Other ancient authorities lack *and was carried up into heaven*

they worshiped him, and[q] returned to Jerusalem with great joy; [53]and they were continually in the temple blessing God.[r]

This final part of Luke's gospel is of one piece with the beginning of Luke's other New Testament writing, the Acts of the Apostles. The gospel concludes and Acts begins with Jesus commissioning his followers to bring the good news of God's mercy to the whole world. Then, having entrusted them with this responsibility and assuring them of the coming of the promised Holy Spirit, he ascends to heaven.

..and he said to them, "Thus it is written, that the Messiah is to suffer and to rise from the dead on the third day, and that repentance and forgiveness of sins is to be proclaimed in his name to all nations, beginning from Jerusalem. You are witnesses of these things. And see, I am sending upon you what my Father promised…" 24:46-49

Meditation: After the Ascension, the life of Jesus' followers in the Church is defined by their mission and responsibility to bring the good news of Jesus Christ, crucified and risen, to all and to offer God's mercy to all who repent and accept God's forgiveness. Not only have the followers of Jesus— that includes us who are believers today— received God's mercy, now they are responsible for sharing that mercy with the entire world.

Question: How responsible do I feel about bringing God's mercy into the world?

Let us pray: May we who have come to know the joy and the power of God's mercy at work in our lives be always ready to share it with others. In our words and in our lives, may we bear witness to the good news of salvation in Jesus Christ to a world in need.

q Other ancient authorities lack *worshiped him, and*
r Other ancient authorities add *Amen*

TAKING THE GOSPEL OF MERCY TO HEART

The Gospel according to Saint Luke insistently proclaims the mercy of God. Luke helps us to see the mission of Jesus as a mission of mercy. Luke emphasizes how God's mercy has taken hold of our world and our lives in Jesus Christ. Luke also emphasizes how Jesus calls us to lives of merciful compassion. Luke's gospel, as we have seen, is a rich source for prayer and reflection.

It would be a mistake, however, to limit the gospel of mercy to the pages of a book. In the life of the Church, the gospel of mercy has come alive in countless believers who have lived it in their daily lives. In a particular way, those who are named as saints are examples for all of us to follow the path of mercy.

In our own time, Saint Faustina Kowalska (d. 1938) encouraged devotion to God's mercy. Her experiences and her writings have encouraged a renewed appreciation of God's mercy in our lives. Across history, other saints, who experienced a deep conversion from sin and a turning to God, have also underscored the power of God's mercy at work in their lives and in the lives of those whom God calls to repentance. We can think, for example, of the powerful witness of Saint Augustine (d. 430) and Saint Mary of Egypt (d. 421).

Saint Josephine Bakhita (d. 1947) was enslaved in her native Sudan as an adolescent and young woman, and she was treated mercilessly. Later, she embraced faith in the merciful Jesus. That conversion enabled her to turn the mistreatment she experienced into loving and compassionate care for others.

Other saints have helped us to appreciate the availability of God's mercy through the Sacrament of Penance. Among these are Saint Alphonsus de Liguori (d. 1787), Saint John Vianney (d. 1859) and Saint Pio (Padre Pio) of Pietralcina (d. 1968). They fostered and encouraged a sacramental encounter with the mercy of God in the Sacrament of Penance.

We have a tradition of martyrs of charity who could also be called martyrs of mercy. These are saints who gave their lives in compassionate love for others. For example, Saint Pedro Calungsod (d. 1672) gave his life protecting a Jesuit missionary in Oceania. Saint Maximilian Kolbe (d. 1941) sacrificed his life at Auschwitz for the father of a family.

Merciful outreach to lepers or those suffering from Hansen's disease belongs to the history of the saints. Saint Francis of Assisi (d. 1226) embraced those with leprosy as Jesus did in the gospels. Closer to our time, Saint Damian de Veuster of Molokai (d. 1889) and Saint Marianne Cope (d. 1918) gave their lives in compassionate service to those with leprosy in the settlement of Kalaupapa in the Hawaiian Islands.

Many saints extended God's merciful care to the sick. Two notable saints who did so with constancy and complete generosity were Saint John of God (d. 1550) and Saint Camillus (d. 1614).

Saint Vincent de Paul (d. 1660) not only cared for the poor whom he called "the friends of God," but also inspired many men and women to help the poor.

Finally, counted among saints across two thousand years are many women who brought God's mercy directly to the poor, women such as Saint Elizabeth of Hungary (d. 1231), Saint Frances of Rome (d. 1440), and Blessed Teresa of Calcutta (d. 1997). Other women brought God's mercy to others in specific ways: by offering education to poor children—Saint Elizabeth Ann Seton (d. 1821); by caring for immigrants—Saint Frances Xavier Cabrini (d. 1917); by caring for Native Americans and African-Americans—Saint Katherine Drexel (d. 1955).

The gospel of mercy proclaimed in the Church is one. The manifestations, the expressions, and the lived reality of that gospel are many. This fact inspires each of us in our own lives to take up and live the mercy of God—in our own way, in our own time, in response to the needs we encounter.

In the end, the mercy of God extended to us and the mercy of God working through us leads us to praise and thank God. We echo Paul's words:

But God, who is rich in mercy, out of the great love with which he loved us even when we were dead through our trespasses, made us alive together with Christ—by grace you have been saved—and raised us up with him and seated us with him in the heavenly places in Christ Jesus, so that in the ages to come he might show the immeasurable riches of his grace in kindness toward us in Christ Jesus. (Eph 2:4-7)

....

For further study:

If you wish to consult a more detailed commentary on Luke's gospel for your personal study, I would recommend Luke Timothy Johnson's reliable and insightful commentary *The Gospel of Luke* in the *Sacra Pagina Series* (Collegeville, MN: The Liturgical Press, 1991).

Acknowledgements:

As I developed this prayer commentary on Luke's gospel, many people helped me with their suggestions and encouragement. In a particular way, I want to acknowledge Joyce Duriga whose editorial hand helped so much to make this a clearer and more readable book. I am also grateful to Deacon Keith Strohm and Elizabeth Johnson of the Archdiocesan Office for the New Evangelization for their dedicated work in seeing this commentary produced from start to finish. Thank you.